HOW TO RUN A BUSINESS IN THE UNITED KINGDOM
A comprehensive guide
to forming and operating
a company
as a foreigner

Simone Domenico Casadei Bernardi

Published by Business Harbour Press,
a trading style of European Business Advisory Ltd.,
a company registered in England and Wales
with Company number 08168291
40 Bloomsbury Way, London, United Kingdom, WC1A 2SE
www.europeanbusinessadvisory.co.uk

All rights reserved. No part of this work may be reproduced or stored in an information retrieval system (other than for purposes of review), without the express permission of the publisher in writing.

The right of Simone Domenico Casadei Bernardi to be identified as author of this work has been asserted by him in accordance with the Copyright, Designs and Patents Act 1988.

First edition published 2018
© Business Harbour Press 2018

British Library Cataloguing in Publication Data
A catalogue record for this book is available from the British Library

ISBN 978-1-73121-285-6
Printed and bound in the European Union

All information was believed to be correct as of 30th October 2018. Whilst every effort has been made to ensure the accuracy of information presented, the author and the editor disclaim all responsibility for and accept no liability for any errors or losses caused by any inaccuracies in this publication or the consequences of any person acting or refraining from acting or otherwise relying on such information. They do not assume any liability for the information contained herein, its interpretation or for any reliance on it.
This book should not be construed as a recommendation, endorsement, opinion or approval of any kind. It has been produced for information only and should not be relied on for legal purposes. Professional advice should always be sought before taking action based on the information provided.

This book is dedicated to my mother
Anna Maria, *in memoriam*, and my father David.
They will always be the kind of person
I yearn to become.

"There is nothing so bad or so good that you will not find an Englishman doing it; but you will never find an Englishman in the wrong. He does everything on principle."

George Bernard Shaw, *The Man of Destiny*

Contents

PREFACE **1**

THE UNITED KINGDOM: AN OVERVIEW **5**
Geography and climate................................... 5
Population and language................................ 6
Transport infrastructure................................ 7
Political system... 8
Legal system.. 10

GENERAL ECONOMIC DATA **13**
Economy and currency 13
Doing business in the United Kingdom 14
The United Kingdom's prevalent business sectors 16
Business legal structures in the United Kingdom 18
        Sole trader... 18
        General partnership 19
        Limited partnership 20
        Limited liability partnership........... 21
        Limited company 21
        Social enterprise 23
Getting professional help.............................. 24

LIMITED COMPANIES IN DETAIL.................27
Memorandum and articles of association...27
Company name...27
Company address 31
Share capital and shareholders 32
Persons with significant control 33
Company management..................................35
Company secretary..37
Standard Industrial Code 38
The incorporation process 38
Confirmation statement................................39
Dealing with Companies House 39
Buying an existing company.........................41

THE BANKING SYSTEM IN THE UNITED KINGDOM...43
British banks..43
How to open a business bank account........45
Dealing with banks as a foreigner................45

ACCOUNTING AND REPORTING...................47
Applicable accounting principles.................47
Financial statements 49

BUSINESS LAW IN THE UNITED KINGDOM
....53
Intellectual property 53
Trade and competition..................................54
Dispute resolution...55
Regulated industries 56
Business permits 62
Late payments...64

British business law and Brexit 66

TAXATION IN THE UNITED KINGDOM 67
Corporation tax 67
VAT in the United Kingdom 69
National Insurance contributions 71
Capital gains 72
Real estate taxation 73
Withholding tax 73
Taxation of individuals 74

IMPORT AND EXPORT 77
Some figures 77
Customs duties 79

LABOUR LAW AND LABOUR COSTS 81
Employment law 81
Working hours 82
Paid vacation 83
Anti-discrimination rules 84
Maternity and parental leave 87
Termination of employment 89
Wage regulation 92
Social insurance system 93

BUSINESS ETIQUETTE IN THE UNITED KINGDOM 95
Punctuality 95
Gift giving 96
Dress code 97
Corporate and social responsibilities 98
Bribery 99

Meetings *99*
Humour *100*
Introductions *100*
Socialisation *101*
Indirect speech *102*

CONCLUSION 105

Annex – Model Articles for private companies limited by shares 107

PREFACE

Starting a new business can be a daunting task, and certainly one that should not be taken likely. However, there are a few simple things to remember. The first key is to ensure that one is launching a business within the appropriate legal structure. If choosing to operate as a sole trader or a partnership, the rest of setting up and sustaining the business is quite simple. Though if one wishes to incorporate a business as a limited company, it becomes more complicated with additional legislation and key dates to bear in mind for submitting financial and administrative statements.

    This book is intended to provide you with an overview to starting and sustaining a new business in the United Kingdom. Whilst there may be challenges to face, an understanding of the content of this book will enable you to be in the position when joining the United Kingdom's economy.

Included is a basic overview of the country, along with business law and information about taxation and trade.

The United Kingdom has been a centre of world trade and business for centuries. In most recent times, it remains an important country in terms of international commerce. It is a migration hub, where people from a wealth of different backgrounds and experiences meet, work together, and co-exist. Regarding communications, many of the world's submarine fibre cabling systems have central points in the United Kingdom, enabling online communication and trade to flow more smoothly. The country also has broad links with other parts of the world, such as the other twenty-seven Member States of the European Union; the fifty-three members of the Commonwealth; the fourteen British Overseas Territories; and the other sixty-six countries with English as the official language.

Which taxes are pertinent to which business types are discussed at length in a dedicated chapter. This is a particularly important topic, as running afoul of such regulations can be financially very costly.

Much of the content relates to laws that are overseen by the European Union. However, some of the information in this book may change from around March 2019 when the UK leaves the European Union. At the moment, nobody can define precisely what these changes may look like, but some likely scenarios are discussed in this book.

HOW TO RUN A BUSINESS IN THE UNITED KINGDOM

THE UNITED KINGDOM: AN OVERVIEW

Geography and climate

The United Kingdom is a country consisting of four coequal parts: England, Scotland, Wales, and Northern Ireland. The *de facto* capital city is London, though Scotland, Wales, and Northern Ireland each have their own capitals also. Certainly, London is the principal city for trade and commerce within the United Kingdom.

The climate of the country is temperate and seasonal, with an annual rainfall of almost nine hundred millimetres. The temperature ranges from an average of 5°C in January to 19°C in July. The variability of precipitation and temperature enabled the development of an agricultural variety in the country, which is one of the reasons for its early growth in the world of trade.

Although latitudinally the United Kingdom ought to have a climate closer to that of

Russia or Canada, the oceanic current known as the Gulf Stream, which begins in the Caribbean Sea and heads towards north-western Europe, brings warmer, wetter weather. This is important in creating the milder climate that is experienced in the United Kingdom.

Population and language

The 2011 United Kingdom Census recorded that sixty-three million people live in the United Kingdom. Of those, over nine million live in London; giving the capital city a population density of five thousand two hundred people per square kilometre. The vast majority of the population of the United Kingdom are white British.

The United Kingdom's official religion is Christianity, and churches of all denominations (Catholic, Protestant, Baptist and Methodist) can be found throughout the country. The main other religions are Islam, Hinduism, Sikhism, Judaism and Buddhism.

While there are Celtic-based languages that exist in parts of the United Kingdom (Scotland, Northern Ireland, and Cornwall), the official language of the country is English. In parts of Wales, especially the north and the west, Welsh (Cymraeg) is spoken as a first language instead.

However, due to the ethnic diversity that the United Kingdom now enjoys, there are a great many languages spoken. For example, in schools in London, it is estimated that over three-hundred different languages are used; the most established of which, aside from English, being Bengali, Gujarati, Punjabi, Cantonese, and Mandarin, because of mass-migration from Asia.

Migration to the United Kingdom has brought a variety of different cultures, customs, and languages to the country. The largest migrant group to the United Kingdom is Indian, followed by Polish. Many restaurants, shops and other services exist in the United Kingdom due to such migration. There are areas in major cities (such as London, Manchester, and Birmingham) in which the local populations speak the language of their home country. While most Britons see this migration as being of benefit to enhance and vary their society, there are sporadically racial tensions between different groups of people.

Transport infrastructure

The United Kingdom has a strong transport infrastructure with a relatively large motorway network for road transport between key commercial centres to air and seaports;

there is also an extensive rail network. Every location within the country is within 100 miles of a container port.

Air travel continues to develop within the United Kingdom through a strong network of regional airports. The UK also has four "Gateway" airports – Heathrow and Gatwick in London, Manchester in the north of England and Glasgow in Scotland. Stansted and Luton are also extensively used, being relatively close to London.

Political system

Broadly speaking, the United Kingdom operates within the bounds of a typical democracy. Though the system is under the jurisdiction of a constitutional monarchy, currently meaning that Queen Elizabeth II is the head of state. However, in real terms, the national mechanisation is presided over by the head of government, the Prime Minister.

Scotland, Wales, and Northern Ireland each hold their own devolved governments, but they are ultimately responsible to the parliament of the United Kingdom, based in London.

The legislative power of the British parliament is entrusted to two chambers, the House of Commons and the House of Lords. Members of Parliament, within the House of Commons, are elected to their position by constituent members of the public within their electoral area. Ninety members of the House of Lords are hereditary peers, elected by themselves and other two are *ex-officio* members; all the other members of the upper house are appointed.

A multi-party system operates within the politics of the United Kingdom. There are two primary parties: the Labour party, who are predominantly typified as left-centrist; and the Conservative party, who are mostly right-centrist. Other parties have been used to form governments with each of these main parties in the past. The current government, for example, is primarily a Conservative one, but Members of Parliament from the Democratic Unionist Party (DUP) of Northern Ireland have favoured the formation of an overall majority.

For a British general election, the "first-past-the-post method" means that once a party gains the majority of seats within the House of Commons, that party has won the election. Their party leader will become Prime Minister. In the case of a no majority result, a coalition will need to be formed lest the country is in a state of "hung parliament", whereby no political party has overall control. This can result in inter-party squabbling and difficulty in getting legislation past the House of Commons.

Legal system

English law is known as the mother of the common law and is based on those principles. Very simplistically, the common law is a system of law which is based on judges' decisions and on custom, rather than on written laws as it happens in the civil law jurisdictions.

There are three legal systems within the United Kingdom, each pertaining to a different geographical area. The largest of these is the English and Welsh Law, where the court system is headed by the Senior Courts of England and Wales: the Court of Appeal; the High Court of Justice – for civil cases; and the Crown Court – for criminal cases.

The Northern Irish Law system follows the same pattern in Northern Ireland. However, the Scots Law, in Scotland, utilises the Court of Session for civil cases, the High Court of Justiciary for criminal cases, and Sherriff Courts for both criminal and civil cases.

Though these three systems contain differences within the details of their laws and how they are administered, there are over-arching systems in place for the whole of the United Kingdom.

The highest court in the country is the Supreme Court of the United Kingdom. Immigration courts, such as the Asylum and Immigration Tribunal and the Special Immigration Appeals Commission, operate across the United Kingdom. The Employment Appeal Tribunal has jurisdiction throughout the United Kingdom, apart from in Northern Ireland.

Moreover, the Judicial Committee of the Privy Council exists as the highest court of appeal for many countries within

- the British Commonwealth (fifty-three countries that have autonomous politics, but use the British Head of State as their official Head of State, too);
- the British Overseas Territories (fourteen areas, mostly island archipelagos, that are the remnants of the British Empire); and
- the British Crown Dependencies (three places off the coast of the British mainland: the Bailiwick of Jersey; the Bailiwick of Guernsey, including the islands of Guernsey, Alderney, and Sark; and the Isle of Man.)

Currently, laws of the European Union are acting within the legal systems of the United Kingdom. However, this may change as the country moves towards a political and legal position outside of the European Union over the coming months and years.

HOW TO RUN A BUSINESS IN THE UNITED KINGDOM

GENERAL ECONOMIC DATA

Economy and currency

The currency used in the United Kingdom is the Pound sterling (GBP), which is the fourth largest reserve currency in the world.

The economy is market-oriented, and the fifth largest in the world, based on gross domestic product, which was equivalent to $2.622 trillion (£2.021tn or €2.302tn circa) in 2017. The United Kingdom's economy comprises approximately three and a half per cent of the world's gross domestic product.

The United Kingdom is the tenth largest goods exporter in the world and the fifth largest good importer. The globalisation of the British economy has meant that the United Kingdom now has the second largest inward foreign direct investment, and the third largest outward foreign direct investment.

The Brexit decision has not yet had a dramatic impact on the amount of foreign direct investment received by the United Kingdom, though there is speculation that this may happen once the country finally withdraws from the European Union. Indeed, the amount received peaked in 2016 and then declined considerably in 2017, but 2018 has seen a re-balancing. The majority of foreign direct investment that comes into the United Kingdom is to the financial business sector.

Membership of various international organisations has meant that the United Kingdom has become significant in global economic systems. Such organisations include the Commonwealth, the European Union (currently), the G7, the G20, the International Monetary Fund, the Organisation for Security and Co-operation in Europe, the World Bank, the World Trade Organisation, the Asian Infrastructure Investment Bank, and the United Nations.

Doing business in the United Kingdom

According to the World Bank Group, the country is currently ranked ninth in the world for ease-of-doing-business. The ranking ranges from 1 to 190 and is updated yearly. The "Ease of Doing Business" index measures regulations directly affecting businesses.

The World Bank Group deeply analyses specific topics, in which the United Kingdom ranks. The rankings are determined by sorting the aggregate scores on 10 topics, each consisting of several indicators, giving equal weight to each topic.

UK: DB 2019 Ease of Doing Business Score

Overall	9
Starting a Business	19
Dealing with Construction Permits	17
Getting Electricity	7
Registering Property	42
Getting Credit	32
Protecting Minority Investors	15
Paying Taxes	23
Trading across Borders	30
Enforcing Contracts	32
Resolving Insolvency	14

Further, the state is ninth in the world when measured on purchasing power parity, and has seen a gross domestic product growth of 1.8 per cent over the last fiscal year (which, in the United Kingdom, runs from the sixth of April until the following fifth of April).

The UK's Office for National Statistics issues an "Annual Survey of Hours and Earnings" (ASHE). According to its latest data, the median full-time yearly earning is £29,588, which approximately equates to €33,701 or to US$38,389. Recent findings show that almost 90 per cent of women work for companies that pay them less than male colleagues.

The labour force of the United Kingdom is 32.4 million, with an employment rate of seventy-six per cent. There are 1.36 million unemployed adults in the country, which has led, in part, to fifteen per cent of the population being below the poverty line.

Exports from the United Kingdom, predominantly manufactured goods, fuels, and chemicals, were worth US$412.1 billion (£317.6 billion or €361.8 billion circa) in 2016. The majority (forty-four per cent) of exported goods go to European Union member states. The same is true of imports, where fifty-three per cent of imports to the United Kingdom are from the European Union. Imports in 2016, mainly manufactured goods, machinery, and foodstuffs, were worth US$581.6 billion (£448.3bn or €510.6bn circa).

The United Kingdom's prevalent business sectors

Approximately eighty per cent of the United Kingdom's gross domestic product is from the service sector. Therefore, such businesses are often profitable, dependent upon specific competition. Finance industries thrive in the United Kingdom, and London is the world's largest financial centre.

Research and development into pharmaceuticals are also successful, with the United

Kingdom's pharmaceutical industry being recognised as the tenth largest globally.

Energy facilities perform well also, predominantly oil and natural gas from the North Sea reserves. However, the largest employer in the United Kingdom, and indeed in the whole of Europe, is the National Health Service. Businesses that maintain a link with this public healthcare sector have proven to be successful.

Creative industries have grown by an average of six per cent a year between 1997 and 2005. The two most massive creative industry clusters in Europe are located in the United Kingdom (London and North-West England). These industries involve businesses that work in sectors such as fashion, music, design, publishing, technology, crafts, computer games, arts, architecture, advertising, television, and film. However, of those, the fastest growing are advertising businesses, due mainly to the advent of digital marketing and social media.

London is the second most visited city in the world, with eighteen million visitors a year. Tourism is vital to the British economy, with over thirty-three million tourists visiting the country annually, contributing over eight per cent to the country's gross domestic product. Industries within, or contributing to, the tourist sector often achieve well.

Business legal structures in the United Kingdom

A legal structure defines the way a business is organised and determine the legal obligations both for the business itself and for its people.

Certain initial business structures can be changed to better suit the business' needs. Further, some legal structures are more popular than others for early-stage businesses, but this paragraph covers the most common ones.

SOLE TRADER

Sole traders are people who own and run their own business. The British law puts upon them the least regulations.

Risks with this structure are the unlimited personal liability of the owner, and the potential dissolution of the business if the owner were to die. If a sole trader trades under a different name to their actual name, they are legally required to display their personal name as the owner, along with an address, on all stationery.

Sole traders don't register themselves with Companies House but they still need to file a tax return to pay Income Tax, and potentially National Insurance Contributions (NIC) and VAT. They can do this through the HMRC's self-assessment. The business' income is taxed as personal income against the individual owner.

> **Companies House**
> Companies House incorporates and dissolves limited companies, and registers company information and makes it available to the public. It is the British counterpart of the Irish "Companies Registration Office", or of the French "Registre du commerce et des sociétés", or of the German "Handelsregister" or of the Italian "Camera di Commercio". Companies House employs more than 1,000 staff.

> **HM Revenue and Customs (HMRC)**
> HMRC is the UK's tax, payments and customs authority. Its 56,000 employees collect the money that pays for the UK's public services and helps families and individuals with financial support. Established by Act of Parliament in 2005, HMRC replaced the Inland Revenue and Customs and Excise.

GENERAL PARTNERSHIP

Within a partnership, each partner becomes an agent who can individually hire employees, borrow money, and operate the business. The partners, or agents, are still personally liable for debts and taxes within the partnership, and profits are again taxed as personal income.

All the partners usually sign a "Partnership Agreement", a document which defines how the ownership, profits and liabilities are divided. With regard to the latter topic, the principle of joint and various other liability of partners of a partnership apply: a third party could address his claims to a single partner for the recovery of the entire debt. Hence, the importance of the "Partnership Agreement", to enable the called-in partner to recover the amount paid from all the other partners.

General partnerships don't register with Companies House. Each partner must register with HMRC as self-employed, and is responsible for the payment of his/her taxes. The partnership is requested to file a self-assessment tax return at the end of each tax year.

LIMITED PARTNERSHIP

A limited partnership is similar to a general partnership, but is subject to the obligation to identify at least one "general partner" and one "limited partner".

A "general partner" is responsible for managing the business. He/she is responsible for all the partnership's debt. On the contrary, a "limited partner" is liable for an amount of debt that equals his/her initial investment and has no management responsibilities. Both general partners and limited partners will need to file individual tax returns and pay NI contributions, if their income exceeds the threshold, via HMRC's self-assessment.

Limited partnerships must register with the Companies House. In Scotland, limited partnerships are a separate legal entity and distinct from their partners, whereas in England and Wales they're not a separate legal entity.

LIMITED LIABILITY PARTNERSHIP

A limited liability partnership (LLP) is a separate legal entity and distinct from its partners. Each partner is liable up to the amount of money he/she initially invested and has management responsibility. Usually, each partner's responsibilities are identified in an "LLP Agreement".

LLPs need to register with Companies House. Further, HMRC should be informed and at the end of each tax year, a partnership self-assessment tax return must be filed. Each partner will need to file an individual tax return and pay NI contributions (if he/she meets the threshold) via HMRC's self-assessment.

LIMITED COMPANY

Limited companies are owned by shareholders, who invest a certain amount of money in return for a share of the business. The company is legally separated from the shareholders, which aren't personally responsible for its debts.

Limited companies can be divided into three categories:

- Private companies limited by shares. Most limited companies are of this type. Each shareholder is liable up to the nominal value of his/her shares. Unless they are also shareholders and assuming they work within the bounds of the law, directors are not financially liable for any debt.
- Private companies limited by guarantee. This structure is mostly used for charities, community projects, clubs, societies and other similar bodies. A company limited by guarantee doesn't have a share capital and the shareholders are replaced by the members (one or more). A company limited by guarantee, as a private company, must have at least one director.
- Public limited company. Like a private company limited by shares, a public limited company is subject to additional requirements including share capital obligations. The company's shares

may be available to be traded on stock exchanges.

Limited companies need to register with Companies House and, generally speaking, they could be more attractive to potential external investors than sole traders or partnerships.

Many international businessmen express their interest toward limited companies, therefore more detailed information about them is provided in the following chapter.

SOCIAL ENTERPRISE

Social enterprises are businesses which blend profit with social purpose. They can be for profit, and operate in a similar way to limited companies. The main difference is that social enterprises need to have a goal which will benefit society, a community, or the wider good. They also have certain operational restrictions.

To qualify as a social enterprise:
- The entity must have a clear mission statement;
- The majority of its income must come from trading;
- The majority of its profits must be reinvested;
- Its social mission must be its top priority; and
- Its business and accounts must be transparent.

Social enterprises which are limited companies can also register with Companies House as a "community interest company" (CIC), to ensure that their assets are dedicated to the public benefit. Companies House provides a bespoke model constitution, with a memorandum of association and articles of association templates. The text of the latter is reproduced in the Annex.

Getting professional help

It is important to avoid errors and misjudgements before they happen, and the most successful entrepreneurs are always ready to listen to sound advice.

To identify the legal structure that fits your needs (and your plans) it is the best to seek out the right professional advisers as early as possible. Accountants, financial planners and lawyers can be of invaluable help.

In the United Kingdom, the term "accountant" does not have the same legal protection as that given to other professions, such as doctors and lawyers. But even if an accountant can be such without any formal qualification, it is advisable to find an accountant who is a member of a recognised association. Among the main professional organisations, the following are some of the ones granted with a royal charter:

- The Institute of Chartered Accountants in England and Wales (ICAEW);
- The Institute of Chartered Accountants of Scotland (ICAS);
- The Association of Chartered Certified Accountants (ACCA);
- The Chartered Institute of Management Accountants (CIMA).

The cost for their advice should be discussed and agreed before any work is carried out.

Financial planners may support a company with its budget projections. It is difficult to choose one, but most large accountancy and business consultancy companies have specialist sections. They usually charge a flat fee, agreed in advance.

Finally, lawyers are particularly useful in advising on the legal form of a new business, the formation process, any contract the business may enter into, etcetera. Their costs vary, but they usually give the client an estimate or a package deal.

LIMITED COMPANIES IN DETAIL

Memorandum and articles of association

When they register their limited company, the shareholders need a "Memorandum of association" and the "Articles of association".

The "Memorandum" is a legal statement signed by all the initial shareholders. The "Memorandum" can't be updated once the company has been registered.

The "Articles of association" are the rules about running the company agreed by the shareholder(s), director(s) and, in some cases, the company secretary. Here again, Companies House provides a standard template (known as "model articles"), the adoption of which is mandatory if the shareholders want to register their company online.

Company name

The shareholders must choose a name for their business if they want to set up a private limited company. The name usually ends in either "Limited" or "Ltd". The Welsh suffix equivalent ("Cyfyngedig" or "Cyf") can be used if the company is registered in Wales.

The shareholders are free to choose the company name, but:

- It can't be the same as (or too similar to) another registered company's name;
- It can't be offensive;
- It can't contain a "sensitive" word or expression; and
- It can't suggest a connection with government or local authorities (unless a permission is granted).

Concerning proper names, there are a great many terms that either cannot be included or must be reviewed before being included, in a company's name.

The following is a list of words and terms that may be used, but that will require permission from the Secretary of State before they can be used:

accredit, accreditation, accredited, accrediting, adjudicator, association, assurance, assurer, audit commission, auditor general, audit office, bank, banking, benevolent, Britain, British, chamber of commerce, chamber of business, chamber of enterprise, chamber of industry, chamber of trade, chamber of training, charitable, charity, charter, chartered, child maintenance, child support, commission, community benefit society, comptroller, co-operative, council, dental, dentistry, dentist, dental surgeon, Duke, Duchess, England, English, federation, financial conduct authority, foundation, friendly society, fund, government, health and safety executive, health and social care board, health centre, health service, health visitor, His Majesty, Her Majesty, House of Commons, House of Lords, HPSS, HSC, inspectorate, institute, institution, insurance, insurer, judicial appointment, King, law commission, licensing, medical centre, midwife, midwifery, mutual, National Assembly, National Audit Office, NHS, Northern Ireland, Northern Irish, nurse, nursing, Office for Nuclear Regulation, ombudsman, parliament, parliamentarian, parliamentary, patent, patentee, Pensions Advisory Service, police, polytechnic, Post Office, Prince, Princess, Prudential Regulation Authority, Public Health Agency, Queen, reassurance, reassure, registrar, registered society, regulator, reinsurance, reinsurer, royal, royalty, Scotland, Scottish, Sheffield, social service, society, special school, standards, stock exchange, trade union, tribunal, trust, underwrite, underwriting, university, Wales, Welsh, Windsor.

For any of these terms used in Welsh (Cymraeg), rather than English, the same rules apply. For example, a company that provides solutions to vandalism and theft by security measures geared to the customer can be named "John Doe Security Ltd.", but the proposed name "Police Security Systems Ltd." will likely be refused by Companies House.

The following list is words or terms that may be used, but may need permission from another body:

accounting council, actuarial council, audit and assurance council, corporate reporting council, agency, assembly, border agency, border force, cabinet office, crime squad, criminal intelligence service, Crown Estate, employment medical advisory service, further education, higher education, HMRC, Home Office, industrial and provident society, intellectual property, Lord Advocate, notary, notarial, nuclear installation, Office of the Public Guardian, primary education, registered society, revenue and customs, scrivener, secondary education, select committee, serious organised crime.

For full details of whom to apply to, if necessary, access the Companies House website. Again, if any of these expressions are used in Welsh instead, they may well still need to be applied for.

The final set of words or terms that are regulated are as follows:

Anzac, architect, bachelor of medicine, building society, chemist, druggist, pharmaceutical, pharmaceutist, pharmacist, pharmacy, chiropractic, chiropractor, chiropractor, Citius, Altius, Fortius, commonhold association, contact lens, credit union, optician, optometrist, doctor of medicine, faster higher stronger, general practitioner, Geneva Cross, Olympic, Olympian, Olympiad, Paralympic, Paralympian, Paralympiad, ordinance survey, physician, Red Crescent, Red Cross, red lion and sun, social worker, solicitor, spirit in motion, surgeon, vet, veterinary.

Company address

The company address ("registered office") is where statutory mail (i.e. letters from Companies House or HMRC) is sent.

The company address must be:

- A physical address in the United Kingdom;

- In the same country, the company is registered in (i.e. a company registered in Scotland must have a registered office in that country).

Share capital and shareholders

When registering their company, information about the shares (known as a "statement of capital") must be provided. This includes:

- The number of shares of each type the company has, and their total value (known as the company's "share capital");
- The names and addresses of all shareholders.

Shareholders are individuals or corporate bodies who legally own one or more shares of stock in a business. Broadly speaking, there are no restrictions on the residency of the shareholders. Whatever their share, a shareholder will be entitled to that proportion of a business' increase in stock valuation. Conversely, they will also have to accept a proportional loss should the business' stock reduce in value.

The share capital is the long-term source of finance for businesses and is generated by money being invested by the shareholders. It is ordinarily used for initial set-up costs, or for ongoing development and expansion of the business.

Legally speaking, there is no minimum value of share capital for a private limited company, though all limited companies must issue at least one share. However, public limited companies do have to issue a minimum share capital value of £50,000.

Until the first of October 2009, there was a maximum limit to the number of shareholders a business could have, referred to as authorised share capital. However, a limited company can now have as many shareholders as they like, so long as the equity of the shareholders is justified.

Persons with significant control

A person with significant control (PSC) (sometimes called "beneficial owner") is someone who owns or controls a company.

Most PSCs are likely to be people who hold:

- more than 25% of shares in the company
- more than 25% of voting rights in the company
- the right to appoint or remove the majority of the board of directors.

A PSC might influence or control the company through other means. This could be directly, or on behalf of someone else. For example, someone who tells the directors or shareholders what to do. In any case, this last condition will only apply in limited circumstances.

PSCs need to be disclosed due to the Small Business, Enterprise and Employment Act 2015, which brought changes to the existing Companies Act 2006. The aim is to provide a higher level of transparency in the control and ownership of British businesses and to help to fight against money laundering.

From the time of the incorporation, the details of the company's PSCs must be disclosed with Companies House and recorded them in the company's PSC register. These details are:

- the name;
- the date of birth;
- the nationality;
- the country of residence;
- the usual residential address.

Further, the conditions of control that each PSC meets and the date he/she became a PSC must be recorded.

The law encourages compliance and self-policing through a combination of legal action and company-imposed sanctions, as briefly summarised on the following page.

Legal Responsibilities for Companies:

Failure to register	£1,000
Failure to take reasonable steps to identify PSCs	Maximum of 2 years in prison and/or a fine

Legal Responsibilities for PSCs:

Failure to respond	Imprisonment or a fine
Failure to notify	Imprisonment or a fine
Failure to update information	Imprisonment or a fine
Failure to provide accurate information	Imprisonment or a fine

In addition to the legal ramifications listed above, the law also empowers companies to restrict the shares or business rights of any person or entity it feels is blocking its ability to faithfully complete its PSC Register. As the last resort, it is possible for a company to sell restrict interest if these sanctions do not lead to positive outcomes.

Company management

The directors of a limited company are required to follow all rules set out in the articles of association. They also have to keep company records and report any changes to the business. The directors are overall responsible for filing accounts and the annual Company Tax Return. They must pay corporation tax, and complete a personal self-assessment tax return each year.

Of course, other people (such as accountants) can be hired to complete these tasks, but the director is still ultimately responsible.

A director can be both a natural person (aged at least 16) or a legal entity, without restrictions on their residency. The law requires at least one director to incorporate a private company limited by shares.

A director has a duty to exercise independent judgment and is required to not use his/her position to make profits at the company's expense. Directors are also legally obliged to declare any actual or potential conflict of interest in the company: for example, if the director has interests in another company with which their company is planning to do business.

In exercising their powers, directors are required to exhibit "such a degree of skill as may reasonably be expected" from a person with a similar knowledge and experience. Further, directors must exercise a degree of care in their actions. The test of an "acceptable level of care" is what a reasonable person would o in looking after their own affairs.

Company secretary

A significant role in company management is that of the company secretary (usually referred to as the corporate secretary in American businesses). This person has responsibility for all administration of the company and the efficient running thereof.

It is neither a clerical nor a secretarial role. Instead, the company secretary is to ensure that the business is compliant to all statutory and regulatory requirements. They are also accountable for guaranteeing that any decisions made by the directors are implemented accurately.

The company secretary will be the named person on any legal documentation pertaining to the business. It is they who must register and communicate with all shareholders and people with significant control. Company records including, but not limited to, the annual accounts produced, are also the responsibility of the company secretary.

Even if there is no need to appoint a company secretary, some companies, especially those managed by foreigners without an experience of business in the United Kingdom, use them to take on some of the directors' responsibilities.

Standard Industrial Code

The business' Standard Industrial Code (SIC) is used to identify the type of business carried on by each company. This will be a five-digit number. Full lists of SICs can be found on the Companies House website.

It is possible to be classified with more than one code if the business is particularly complex. However, no more than four SICs can be used for any one company.

The incorporation process

Once all is prepared, the simplest way for a business to register as being limited is online, using the United Kingdom's government website (www.gov.uk). The process usually takes twenty-four hours to process.

Alternatively, the company can be registered by post using the form "IN01".

Once the company is officially formed, Companies House will issue a "Certificate of incorporation", that attributes the company a "company number". At the same time, HMRC will issue the company's Unique Tax Reference (UTR), which is then used by the business when registering for corporation tax, using PAYE when employing staff, and for VAT-related purposes.

Confirmation statement

Once every twelve months from its incorporation, each limited company in the United Kingdom needs to file a confirmation statement with Companies House. It confirms the company's information is up to date.

Failure to file the confirmation statement is a criminal offence which can result in a late filing penalty and the directors being fined in the criminal courts. Failure to pay the late filing penalty can result in enforcement proceedings. The registrar may also take steps to strike the company off the public record.

Dealing with Companies House

There are certain changes to a business that shareholders must approve of in advance. These changes must be notified to Companies House, in most cases through its online service.

Amendments to be reported to Companies House include:
- the business' name;
- the directors and the company secretaries or their personal details or the removal of a director;
- the PSCs or their personal details;
- a change to the company's articles of association;

- a change in the company's share structure.

Most such resolutions can be called 'ordinary', meaning that they require only a majority agreement. However, some may require a seventy-five per cent majority, making the resolution be considered to be 'special'.

Some of the changes applying to small companies are listed, together with their relative forms follows:

Occurrence	Form
Appointment of a new director	AP01 or AP02
Termination of appointment of a director	TM01
Change of the details of a director	CH01
Termination of appointment of a director	TM02
Appointment of a new secretary	AP04
Change of the details of a secretary	CH03
Change of registered office	AD01
Change of company name	NM01 or NM04
Alteration to Memorandum and Articles	Copy of the resolution
Application to strike the company off the register	DS01

Finally, it is the directors' responsibility to send the Confirmation Statement to the Registrar on time.

The Confirmation Statement, previously known as Annual Return, confirms or update the information about the company held by Companies House.

A statement must be filed at least once a year. It's a criminal offence not to submit the statement within 14 days of the end of the review period. If the Confirmation Statement is not filed, the company and its officers might be prosecuted. Further, the company may be struck off the register.

Buying an existing company

An alternative to the incorporation of a new company is the purchase of an existing entity. From a legal viewpoint, the transfer of ownership is made through the transfer of shares to the names of the new shareholders and the submission to Companies House of the changes in directors, registered office and company secretary (if appointed).

It must be noted that the company is a legal entity on its own, so when it is bought by someone, the buyer buys its debts and liabilities together with its assets. Hence, many facets must be considered and professional advice must be sought.

HOW TO RUN A BUSINESS IN THE UNITED KINGDOM

THE BANKING SYSTEM IN THE UNITED KINGDOM

British banks

There has historically been a wide range of banks and building societies within the United Kingdom. However, the country's banking sector is now dominated by a select few large groups. The most notable of these are the Lloyds group (with twenty-eight per cent of the market share for current accounts); Barclays; the Royal Bank of Scotland; and HSBC. The merging of different banks has mostly been in response to the financial crisis of 2008, following which there was much consolidation.

It has been noted that a number of these larger banks essentially operate monopolies in the supply of services to small and medium-sized enterprises. This has culminated in a lack of competition, which has made access to banking services worse for customers as they see little point in switching banks when all of them offer very similar costs and benefits.

In comparison to banking in many European Union countries, British banks tend to be a lot more centralised towards major banking brands. Whereas European countries offer access to financial services at a much more bespoke, local level. Lots of them use high street branches as a means of connecting with their local community, rather than being based solely on the corporate brand. They will offer space in the branches for local businesses and showcase arts and culture from the area. As well as that, many European bank branches have hubs of assisted self-service terminals, which go beyond the role of traditional automated teller machines to full digital experiences for the customers.

London is considered to be a major financial hub and is the European base for many FinTech companies. Such businesses are those involved in the increasing use of technology to enhance financial activities; for example, mobile banking apps and cryptocurrency. In the wake of the Brexit decision, many of these companies are likely to seek new office space in a European Union city instead.

In the United Kingdom, the Financial Conduct Authority is responsible for ensuring that financial markets operate in a fair and consistent manner. Banks are subject to stringent regulations and must be able to evidence that they can not only pass any stress test that they are faced with, but also that they play their part in keeping financial markets in a state of competition.

How to open a business bank account

As a British resident, the process of opening a business bank account is quite simple. One would need to have photographic proof of identity for all company directors, and evidence of directors' address. The identity documents that can be used are a passport, a photo driving license, or a national ID card. For proving the address, a recent bank statement, utility bill, or council tax statement (ordinarily from within the last three months) would suffice. Company details such as the business address, Companies House registration number, and estimated annual turnover will also be required.

Dealing with banks as a foreigner

The opening of an UK-based business bank account is one of the most issues foreign entrepreneurs experience when setting up a British company. If the company director and the PSCs don't reside in the United Kingdom and don't have previous agreements with British banks, it's nearly impossible to have a business bank account opened in the country. Fortunately, the applicable law allows the British legal entities to open their bank accounts abroad.

Even if each bank is required to complete a Customer Due Diligence (CDD) before opening an account, the experience shows that applications made to some eastern European banks are more likely to be successful. An alternative is to apply for an account with a money transfer service or a payment solution provider.

While British law allows businesses based in the United Kingdom to have their bank accounts in other countries, the opposite is very difficult. Foreign corporate entities struggle to open business bank accounts in the United Kingdom unless they bank with a large international institution in their home country. In such cases, this bank may be able to assist you in setting up an account on your behalf. The one bank that has a strong reputation for helping smaller international businesses to set up British business bank accounts, albeit on a case by case basis, is HSBC.

ACCOUNTING AND REPORTING

Applicable accounting principles

There are a variety of accounting principles set out by the generally accepted accounting principles, any of which could be applicable to a new business in the United Kingdom. While the definitions, and even the titles, of these principles, varies from source to source, the general meaning of them is still valid.

The *economic entity principle*, for example, is applicable to sole traders and to partnerships. In such businesses, the business and personal assets are to be considered as one entity. However, for the purpose of accounting, the business transactions are to be kept separate from the owner's personal transactions.

The period of time being discussed or quantified in any financial statement must be standard to meet the criteria of the *time period principle*. This rule is intended to create a standard set of comparable periods, essential for trend analysis.

In order to meet the *full disclosure principle*, any information that is important to someone using a business' financial statements must be provided either within the statement or in the notes thereof. It is usual for a business to list its accounting policies as the first note with its financial statements.

The *going concern principle* allows a business to defer some of its expenses until future accounting periods, provided that the business will continue to exist long enough to meet its objectives.

Further, according to the *accrual principle*, accounting transactions should be recorded in the accounting period when they actually occur, rather than in the periods when they generate cash flow variations–a revenue must be recorded when the customer is invoiced, rather than when the invoice is paid; a commission must be recorded when the sales representative earns it, rather than when it is paid to him/her.

The above principles and many others with them must be considered together with the *consistency principle*: once an accounting principle is adopted, its adoption must continue until a demonstrably better principle or method comes along. The jump between different accounting treatments of essentially similar transactions would make the business' long-term financial results extremely difficult to discern.

Financial statements

A sole trader is not required to keep either a balance sheet or an income statement, although one may wish to do so for one's own records. Wages for oneself are not included in this for tax purposes. By the end of the fiscal year (generally, the fifth of April in the United Kingdom), sole traders are required to have completed a tax return for HMRC. The tax return needs to show the business' profits and losses, and the amounts needed to be paid as National Insurance and as income tax.

Partnerships have the same regulations about this as sole traders do. Again, a tax return is needed by HMRC by the end of the fiscal year. This should show all profits and losses, as well as the amount required to be paid as National Insurance and as income tax.

The annual tax return must be completed and submitted to HMRC by the thirty-first of January each year. The tax return will be based upon the business' finances for the previous fiscal year. Therefore, if a company were submitting a tax return in January 2022, it would be for the financial year from the sixth of April 2020 until the fifth of April 2021.

As with sole traders and partnerships, a tax return is required by HMRC for limited companies. Further, copies of annual statutory accounts also need to be sent to Companies

House. Statutory accounts comprise of the following:

- A balance sheet showing the company's assets, liabilities, and net worth on a stated date;
- A profit and loss account showing the sales, running costs, and the profit or loss the business has made during the financial year;
- Notes about the accounts to explain what is shown; and
- A director's report summarising the economic state of the business over the fiscal year.

These documents must include the director's name, and be signed by the director.

Accounts must be audited unless the business is exempt because it is small. A company may qualify for an audit exemption if it has at least 2 of the following:

- An annual turnover is less than £10.2 million;
- Assets are less than £5.1 million;
- 50 or fewer employees on average.

The auditing is an annual process, and auditors have the right to access the business' accounts at all times. They may also require that anyone accountable for any of the accounts be available to explain any aspects of the accounts.

It is worth noting that it is not the auditors' responsibility to prevent error or fraud; that obligation still lies with the director(s).

BUSINESS LAW IN THE UNITED KINGDOM

Intellectual property
In the United Kingdom, there is no requirement to register a copyright. Copyright is generally reserved for artistic output and will subsist for seventy years from the death of the work's creator. However, trademark infringement is something to be considered by British businesses.

Trademarks are created through registration and last indefinitely. The original trademark registration will last for ten years, but this can be extended by a further ten years each time the protection is coming to an end.

Logos and business names are recommended to be protected by trademark registration. Further, if the business creates an invention, then a patent is advised. Ordinarily, one would appoint a specialist patent agent to assist in this.

The United Kingdom remains a part of the European Patent Organisation and the Patent Cooperation Treaty, and so these are the bodies with whom a patent can be acquired. A patent exists for twenty years following the application date.

If instead, the business has created new designs for a manufactured item, then a registered design right should be used instead. These last for twenty-five years from the registration date.

An unregistered design right can apply to three-dimensional objects and will prevent the commercial replication of such. It is created automatically, without registration, and last for ten years.

Trade and competition

The United Kingdom is subject to both the Competition Act 1998 and the Enterprise Act 2002. Moreover, the European Commission has jurisdiction over competition law within all European Union countries.

The main tasks of the United Kingdom competition are to:

- Prohibit a practice that restricts free trading and business competition;
- Ban practices that lead to domination by a single business; and

- Supervise the merger or acquisition by larger enterprises.

Watchdog agencies exist to maintain competition law, alongside the Office of Fair Trading and the Competition Commission. Such watchdogs include Ofgem (Office of Gas and Electricity Markets), Ofcom (Office of Communications), and Ofwat (Water Services Regulation Authority). Predominantly, watchdog agencies are concerned with the connection between state and privately-owned assets.

Dispute resolution

Though some disputes between consumers and businesses may result in going to court, the government of the United Kingdom actively discourages this. Instead, a process known as ADR (Alternative Dispute Resolution) is preferred. ADR commonly involves either mediation or arbitration. Mediation will include an independent third party who assists the disputatious parties in reaching a mutually acceptable decision. Whereas arbitration will utilise an independent third party to make their own decision, considering all facts presented, which will bind one or both of the parties.

Financial services, energy provision, and the telecoms industry in the United Kingdom already make use of large ADR schemes.

There is legislation in place for the use of ADR, but it is not mandatory for all businesses. However, such entities are required to direct consumers towards an ADR scheme if a dispute cannot be resolved by the business itself.

Alternatively, the European Regulation on Online Dispute Regulation will allow British consumers to resolve disputes over the internet, again without the need for legal action to ensue. It is unconfirmed as to whether or not this will still apply to the United Kingdom's withdrawal from the European Union.

Regulated industries

Businesses which are controlled by government rules are considered to be regulated industries. In the United Kingdom, local authorities, professional associations, and various European regulators provide regulatory functions.

Specific industries which have British government regulation are:

- Charities, which are regulated by:
    - the Charity Commission for England and Wales
    - the Charity Commission for Northern Ireland
    - the Office of the Scottish Charity Regulator)
- Education, which is regulated by:

- the General Teaching Councils for Scotland, Wales, and Northern Ireland
- the Office of Qualifications and Examinations Regulation (Ofqual)
- the Office for Standards in Education, Children's Services and Skills (Ofsted)
- Environmental industries, which are regulated by:
  - the Environment Agency
  - Natural Resources Wales
  - the Northern Ireland Environment Agency
  - the Scottish Environment Protection Agency
- Finance, which is regulated by:
  - the Financial Conduct Authority
  - the Financial Reporting Council
  - the Payment Systems Regulator
  - the Pensions Regulator
  - the Prudential Regulation Authority

- the Office for Professional Body Ani-Money Laundering Supervision
- the Competition and Markets Authority
- Healthcare, which is regulated by:
  - the Care Quality Commission
  - NHS Improvement
  - the Complementary and Natural Healthcare Council
  - the General Chiropractic Council
  - the General Dental Council
  - the General Medical Council
  - the General Osteopathic Council
  - the General Pharmaceutical Council
  - the Health and Care Professions Council
  - Health and Safety Executive
  - the Human Fertilisation and Embryology Authority

- - the Medicines and Healthcare Products Regulatory Agency
  - the Nursing and Midwifery Council
  - the Pharmaceutical Society of Northern Ireland
  - the Professional Standards Authority for Health and Social Care
- Legal businesses, which are regulated by:
  - the Bar Standards Boards
  - CILEx Regulation
  - the Faculty of Advocates
  - the Law Society of Northern Ireland
  - the Law Society of Scotland
  - Master of the Faculties
  - the Office of the Immigration Services Commissioner
  - the Solicitors Regulation Authority
- Social care, which is regulated by:
  - the Scottish Care Inspectorate
  - the Care Council for Wales

- - the General Social Care Council
  - the Northern Ireland Social Care Council
  - the Scottish Social Services Council
- Transport, which is regulated by:
  - the Civil Aviation Authority
  - the Office of Rail and Road
- Utility services, which are regulated by:
  - the Office of Communication (Ofcom)
  - the Phone-paid Services Authority (which is part of Ofcom)
  - the Office for Nuclear Regulation
  - the Office of the Gas and Electricity Markets (Ofgem)
  - the Water Services Regulation Authority (Ofwat)
  - the Utility Regulator
  - the Water Industry Commissioner for Scotland
  - the Council for Registered Gas Installers

- - the Oil and Gas Authority
- Media and marketing businesses, which are regulated by:
  - the Advertising Standards Authority
  - the British Board of Film Classification
  - the Direct Marketing Authority
  - IMPRESS (an independent press regulator)
  - the Independent Press Standards Organisation
- Building and engineering businesses, which are regulated by:
  - the Engineering Council
  - Planning Inspectorate
  - Scottish Housing Regulator.

Other national regulatory bodies include:

- the Equality and Human Rights Commission
- the Independent Police Complaints Commission
- the Security Industry Authority
- the Food Standards Agency
- the Forensic Science Regulator
- the Gambling Commission

- the Gaming Board for Great Britain
- the Gangmasters Licensing Authority.

Business permits

The government of the United Kingdom requires licenses or permits for many aspects of particular businesses. All of them can be applied for using the government's website (www.gov.uk). Some pertain only to specific parts of the United Kingdom.

Some licenses or permits required within the United Kingdom subdivide into different types of licence for different parts of the country. However, the licences or permits that may be commonly necessary for relevant businesses are:

- Child performance licence
- Art therapist registration
- Animal medicine licence
- Pig movement licence
- Food premises approval
- House in multiple occupation licence
- House to house charitable collections licence
- Licence to possess or sell drug precursor chemicals
- Machine Games Duty

- Registration as a waste carrier, broker, or dealer
- Alcohol licensing
- Entertainment licensing
- Oil and gas licensing.

Licenses or permits required within England only are:

- Road occupation licence for building work
- Scrap metal dealer licence
- Skip licence
- Street collection licence
- Street trading licence
- Temporary Events Notice.

Licenses or permits required within Scotland only are:

- Approval for a centre to offer qualifications
- Road occupation licence
- Skip licence.

Licenses or permits required within Wales only are:

- Cattle movement notification
- Road occupation licence for building work
- Scrap metal dealer licence
- Skip licence
- Street collection licence
- Street trading licence
- Temporary Events Notice.

Licenses or permits required within Northern Ireland only are:
- Amusement permit
- Slaughterman licence.

Late payments

Late payments create cash flow problems, which is a cause for concern, especially in today's economy.

In those circumstances, the Late Payment of Commercial Debts (Interest) Act 1998 applies. The law has two purposes. Firstly, to compensate creditors for the late payment of debts and secondly, to deter late payments.

The Act introduces the statutory right to apply interest and compensation to all contracts. The supplier needs to decide whether to enforce this right and if so how. Broadly speaking, the law applies if the agreement doesn't include a specific provision for interest.

According to the law, every business has a statutory right to charge interest on late payments. The right applies to sales to business and public sector customers but doesn't apply to sales to private consumers.

The establishment of an obligation to pay interest starts from the end of the agreed credit period. If the parties have not agreed a period, payment is usually late after 30 days. In any case, the maximum contractual payment period that can be agreed is 60 days.

In those circumstances, the supplier has the right to charge interest at the Bank of England base rate plus 8%. For example, if the base rate is 0.75%, the provider could charge interest at 8.75%.

The base rate is updated twice a year by the Bank of England. Starting with the base rate on 31st December used for debts becoming late between 1st January and 30th June and a second rate in force from 30th June for late payments between 1st July and 31st December.

The creditor is also entitled to claim reasonable debt recovery costs. According to the law, the supplier can claim £40 for debts of less than £1,000, £70 for debts between £1,000 and £10,000 and £100 for debts of £10,000 or more. If the recovery costs are higher than this, the actual costs can be claimed if 'reasonable'.

For example, if your business was owed £1,000, the Bank of England base rate was 0.75%, and the invoice was settled with a 50-day delay, the annual statutory interest on this would be £1,000 x 8.75 / 100 = £87.50. Divide £87.50 by 365 to get the daily interest: £87.50 / 365 = £0.24. After 50 days this would be £12 (£0.24 x 50). The total claim would be £52, given by £12 of interest plus £40 of reasonable debt recovery costs.

British business law and Brexit

At the moment, many aspects of the legislation that relate to business law pertinent to the United Kingdom are borne of European Union laws.

Should the United Kingdom maintain the course to leave through the European Union, such rules might no longer be effective. Ultimately, nobody knows what Brexit may hold for the face of British business, nor for the laws that govern it. The intention, however, is that the aspects of European Union law be entered into British law, for parliament to then decide which parts to retain, modify, replace, or remove.

The Companies Act 2006 itself is partially based on the EU regulations, especially facets related to accounting, information disclosure and the rights of shareholders. It's unlikely that significant changes to these areas will be considered by the government of the United Kingdom.

TAXATION IN THE UNITED KINGDOM

Corporation tax

Corporation tax applies to limited companies, but not to sole traders or partnerships. A limited company must register for corporation tax within three months of its incorporation.

Apart from companies that make profits from oil extraction or oil rights in the United Kingdom, the corporation tax main rate on profits was set at nineteen per cent for the year starting 1st April 2018. This is set to be reduced to seventeen per cent for the year starting 1st April 2020.

Corporation tax is to be paid by a pre-set deadline, which is usually nine months and one day following the end of the business' accounting year. If a business earns profits of over £1.5 million per annum, it usually pays corporation tax in instalments throughout the year. If a business is running at a loss, the business still needs to state that they have nothing to pay officially.

Some costs are not deductible from profits. Amongst the others, some of them are more commonly claimed for expenses:

- Asset depreciation is not a tax-deductible expense, and perceived losses should not be included on tax returns;
- Client entertainment, such as dinner, coffee and drinks, is not deductible as an accounting expense. However, the expenses for the entertainment of the staff can be claimed;
- Customer gifts are not permitted as expenses unless they fall under £50. Food, drink, tobacco and anything that carries an advertisement for your business are completely excluded;
- Legal fees relating to the issue of share capital, or matters of capital items (equipment, property, etc.) are non-tax-deductible expenses. Fees incurred by obtaining loans, patents and registering trademarks are deductible instead;

- Fines or penalties, be they from HMRC or any other governing body, cannot be claimed as expenses.

VAT in the United Kingdom

The standard rate of value added tax (VAT) in the United Kingdom is twenty per cent. This is ordinarily included in the price of products bought, though service-based businesses are likely to add it on as an addition to their fee. Some products are eligible for the lower VAT rate of five per cent. Still, some further products have a zero per cent VAT rate.

Education, finance, insurance, and the services of doctors and dentists are all exempt from VAT. If a business supplies only such exempt supplies and services, they do not have to, and probably are not able to, register for VAT. For supplies and services on the zero per cent rate of VAT, the business may still have to register, or at least apply for exemption from registration. Such goods include food (not including restaurant food or takeaway meals), clothing and shoes for children, medical prescriptions, new residential properties and books and newspapers.

The five per cent VAT rate includes supplies such as children's car seats, fuel and energy used in the home, plus services provided by most charities. The standard rate (twenty per cent) applies to all other supplies and services.

If a business generates over £85,000 per year in VAT-taxable income, that business is obliged to apply for VAT registration. Businesses with a lower income than £85,000 per annum do not need to register for VAT, but can register for VAT voluntarily.

There are severe penalties and fines for attempts, whether they are intentional or not, to evade or delay paying VAT. If a company fails to register for VAT, they will be charged unless there is a reasonable excuse for the delay. The penalty is a percentage of the "potential lost revenue" (PLR) due to failure to register on time, varying from 30% (failure not deliberate) to 100% (delay deliberate and concealed). Further, a default occurs if HMRC has not received all the VAT due on a return by the due date (7 days after the end of the month following the VAT period end). In this case, the company receives a warning called "Surcharge Liability Notice" (SLN): if it fails to pay the VAT due by the due date for any returns due within the next year, the surcharge will be 2% of the outstanding tax. The surcharge increases to 5% for the next default, and then by 5% increments to a maximum of 15%. Special arrangements are offered to small businesses who have a turnover of up to £150,000. This includes sending a letter offering help and support following the first default rather than an SLN. This arrangement is intended to allow extra time to sort out any short-term difficulties before formally entering the default surcharge system. Any further default within twelve months will result in the issue of an SLN.

HMRC is phasing in its landmark Making Tax Digital (MTD) regime, which will ultimately require taxpayers to move to a fully digital tax system. The first area to be affected by MTD will be VAT with the new rules being implemented from April 2019.

Under the regulations, businesses with taxable turnover above the VAT threshold must keep digital records for VAT purposes and provide their VAT return information to HMRC using a "functional compatible software".

National Insurance contributions

National Insurance is a system in the United Kingdom whereby employees and employers contribute towards state benefits and the state pension.

An employee is subject to Class 1 National Insurance payments, which will be deducted directly by the employer. The rates for Class 1 National Insurance payments are zero per cent for earnings less than £702 a month, 12% for earnings between £702 and £3,863 a month, plus an additional 2% for incomes over £3,863 a month.

People who are self-employed, or who are directors of a business, need to pay different rates of National Insurance. Self-employed people need to pay Class 2 and Class 4 National Insurance contributions. Class 2 contributions are charged at the rate of £2.85 per week, regardless of earnings. If the company is earning over £45,000 in profits, this class of National Insurance contributions remains set at the same rate. Class 4 contributions, however, are charged as a percentage of profits. Profits of less than £8,164 are not taxable for class four contributions. A 9% levy is charged for Class 4 contributions on profits between £8,164 and £45,000, and there is an extra 2% charge on any profits above £45,000.

Capital gains

This is a tax against the profit made by selling an asset that has increased in value. Capital gains tax applies to personal possessions worth £6,000 or more, excluding cars, any property that is not one's main home, shares, and business assets.

If capital gains are less than £11,700 during a financial year, no capital gains tax needs to be paid. If a business or individual's taxable gains are within the basic income tax band (see paragraph 7.7), then a rate of 10% (or 18% on residential property) is due. If the taxable gains are within the higher or additional income tax bands, this capital gains tax rate increases to 20% (or 28% on residential property).

Real estate taxation

The sale of real estate in the United Kingdom is subject to capital gains tax (see section 7.4). Stamp duty land tax (SDLT) is payable on the purchase of real estate.

For residential properties, there is a scale of increasing percentages of taxation dependent upon the cost of the property, and whether it is a person's only property or not. For non-residential real estate, SDLT is usually set at 5%, though there is some variation within this.

VAT at 20% may also be charged for the purchase of the non-residential real estate.

Withholding tax

Income tax in respect of recurring payments at source is sometimes collected by requiring the payer to make a deduction on account of income tax before making the payment. This deduction is generally known as "withholding tax".

As a general rule, United Kingdom law requires that businesses that make payments of interest are to pay withholding tax at twenty per cent. There are exclusions to this rule, such as for payments of interest on private placement debts of British companies or payments of interest paid to a British bank.

Royalties, patents, and copyrights are also subject to withholding tax if they have arisen in the United Kingdom. Some treaties exist to allow reduced rates of tax on a variety of royalties.

There is no requirement to deduct WHT from dividends. Therefore, dividends may always be paid gross, regardless of the terms of the applicable double taxation treaty.

Taxation of individuals

The main form of taxation on working individuals in the United Kingdom is income tax. Profits and other taxable income below £11,501 within a fiscal year is not subject to income tax. Profits and other taxable income between £11,501 and £45,000 are subject to the basic income tax rate of twenty per cent. Profits and other taxable income between £45,001 and £150,000 are charged at the higher income tax rate of forty per cent. The additional income tax rate, which is forty-five per cent, is payable on all profits and other taxable income that is over £150,000 within a fiscal year.

For example, if an individual were to generate £160,000 in profits during a financial year, they would pay zero per cent income tax for the first £11,500, the basic rate of twenty per cent income tax on £33,499, the higher rate of forty per cent income tax on £104,999; and forty-five per cent income tax on £9,999 – which is taxed at the additional rate.

Also, individuals need to pay motoring taxes if they own a vehicle which uses public roads.

Finally, inheritance tax is to be paid upon the inheritance of certain items from a deceased donor. This is assessed at forty per cent of the net value of the estate of the departed.

IMPORT AND EXPORT

Some figures

Goods exported from the United Kingdom decreased by 1.3 per cent to £31.2 billion between July 2018 and August 2018. However, August 2018's figure was twenty per cent (£5.2 billion) higher than the same time the previous year. This suggests that, though there are in-year fluctuations, the implications of the United Kingdom's Brexit decision are yet to have an adverse effect on British exports.

Imports to the United Kingdom decreased by 1.2 to £41.5 billion between July 2018 and August 2018. There was also a small decrease (of 0.1 per cent) from August 2017. The United Kingdom remains a net importer, financially speaking. In this recent example, August 2018's imports exceeded exports by £10.3 billion.

Though, when investigating the data more closely, it becomes apparent that perhaps trade between the United Kingdom and the European Union is on the decline. In January 2018, fifty per cent of British exports went to European Union countries. This figure had declined to forty-three per cent by August of the same year. Likewise, imports to the United Kingdom from the European Union fell by eight per cent to forty-nine per cent between February and August 2018.

Trade between the United Kingdom and the United States of America (USA) has increased in recent years. Between 2010 and 2016, British exports to the USA rose from £70.6 billion to £99.6 billion. Over the same period, imports to the United Kingdom from the USA increased from £46.9 billion to £66.3 billion.

Overall, the USA is the highest recipient of British exports, receiving 13.1 per cent of the total. The other countries in the top five of that list are all European Union countries: Germany (10.5 per cent), France (7.4 per cent), Netherlands (6.2 per cent) and the Republic of Ireland (5.7 per cent). In the post-Brexit British economy, currently, there are no known facts in terms of which other countries they will conduct their most trade with. It is likely that the USA will remain top of the list, especially following the current US President's claim that he would like to strengthen and build upon the existing trade between the countries.

Many people suggest that trade with European Union member states will decrease following no deal being made as part of Brexit. Many of the same people also indicate that such trade may start to increase again over coming decades, once the initial market's shock of Brexit has calmed down. As with many other issues surrounding the Brexit debate, there is no confirmed prediction of what the United Kingdom's trading landscape will look like following the country's withdrawal from the European Union.

Customs duties

United Kingdom duty on imported goods varies based on the value of the goods and the type of product that it is. Products are given different duty ratings and thus different percentages of the value. The government of the United Kingdom provides a duty amount checking service online (www.gov.uk/trade-tariff).

As well as UK duty, value-added tax will also need to be paid. VAT is set at twenty per cent in the United Kingdom. The VAT payable on imported goods is not just twenty per cent of the price of the goods, but it is also calculated on the shipping cost and the UK duty payable.

To use an example to demonstrate, if one were to buy an import for the equivalent of

£1,000 and had been charged £200 for shipping and three per cent for UK duty, the first thing to do would be to calculate the duty payable. This would be three per cent of the import's cost, therefore the duty would be £30. The item, shipping, and duty combined would be £1,230. Therefore, the VAT payable would be twenty per cent of that (£246). In total, the tariffs payable on this import would come to £276 – that being £30 in UK duty and £246 in VAT.

LABOUR LAW AND LABOUR COSTS

Employment law
There are a variety of Acts and Regulations in British law that pertain to employment rights. Relationships between employees, employers, and trade unions are regulated and maintained by these laws. Minimum wage laws exist to ensure that employees in the United Kingdom are paid to a suitable living standard (see section 9.7).

In addition to the rights and legislation discussed in the rest of this chapter, employees also have the right to be automatically enrolled in a basic pension, under the Pensions Act 2008. The funds in said pension have to be protected according to the legislation written in the Pensions Act 1995.

Arguably the most important right for employees involved their ability to participate in decision-making for the business and its management collectively. The right to strike may come into place if employees feel that their voices are not being heard. If a company has over fifty staff members, employers are legally obliged to inform and consult their employees about any large-scale economic changes or challenges to the business. Although, it is not a requirement under United Kingdom law for employees to vote for their business' directors.

Should a business be bought by another concern, the Transfer of Undertakings (Protection of Employment) Regulations 2006 will come into force. This process is often known as the acronym TUPE. This set of Regulations means that employees' terms of employment cannot be made worse unless there be a severe organisational or economic reason to do so.

All employers must provide a "safe system of work" to maintain the health and safety of their staff. There have been numerous political Acts about this over the last two centuries, but the one which is still in place is the Health and Safety at Work etc. Act 1974

Working hours

Employees in the United Kingdom are entitled to breaks from work (a minimum of twenty minutes for every six-hours spent working), and a limit to excessively long working hours. Also, the Employment Rights Act 1996 means that employees have a right to leave for childcare and the right to ask their employer to consider flexible working patterns.

The principal legislation in this area in the Working Time Regulations 1998, stipulate a maximum amount of working hours. For instance, if a person works at night-time, they cannot exceed eight working hours in a 24-hour period. Every employee must have a minimum of eleven consecutive hours away from work during a 24-hour period.

Under European Union legislation, no-one may work more than forty-eight hours in a week. However, the United Kingdom government have brought in an opt-out scheme for that, whereby an employee can officially choose to work for longer. In many cases, especially those with lots of additional work that cannot be completed within usual work timings, people may feel socially pressured to complete the same amount of work as their colleagues, and therefore may work for more than forty-eight hours in a week.

Paid vacation

According to the Working Time Regulations 1998, employees are entitled to a minimum of twenty-eight days of paid holiday (vacation) time each year, including public holidays.

Employers are not allowed to offer "rolled up holiday pay", such as additional earnings, instead of the employee taking time off work. This is because the purpose of these regulations is for employees to have actual respite time to promote better mental and physical health. However, if a position is terminated before the employee has used their annual paid holiday allocation, the employer must give additional pay for the unused entitlement.

Anti-discrimination rules

All employees and potential employees must be treated equally. The Equality Act 2010 means that this is the case unless there is a strong justification otherwise. Decisions about, or affecting, employees must not be based on their gender, race, age, beliefs, or sexual orientation. Even if the employer is making a decision with a positive motive, they must remain objective and not consider differences in people, otherwise what they are doing is unlawful.

Should a case of discrimination at work go to court, the claimant would not need to make a comparison with a person of a different gender, race, age, etc. If would be enough, under British law, to compare their treatment to a hypothetical person. There would be no need for the claimant to prove that their employee intended to discriminate, merely that they did so.

There are legal cases when an employer can justify their discrimination. Of course, morally and socially people would agree that no kind of discrimination can be justified. Harassment, for example, legally defined by the Protection from Harassment Act 1997 as being when someone's dignity is violated, or that person is subject to a hostile, degrading, or intimidating environment, cannot lawfully be justified. However, specific roles require that an employee is physically fit, as that a "genuine occupation requirement", and therefore may not offer a position to someone of an advanced age. While this may usually be considered as simply being discrimination, certain workplaces (for example, in the fire and rescue service), may well see that as being justified, and courts would be likely to agree with them.

In terms of justified discrimination, there have been cases in the United Kingdom of people fighting against dismissal, arguing that they were dismissed because of their religion. One such example is of a Christian registrar who refused to register the marriages of a same-sex couple and had her contract terminated for not completing her duties. Courts found in favour of her employer, stating that the equality rights of the citizens' sexual orientation superseded her right to refuse something that was considered wrong according to her religious views. The local authority who dismissed the registrar was aiming to keep to the law of providing their service for anyone regardless of their sexual orientation, and therefore her dismissal was upheld.

In addition to legislation regarding discrimination and equality, employers are bound to do all they can to enable the participation in the business by disabled colleagues. Favourable treatment must be given to disabled people to give them preferential treatment; this is law, though it goes against some of the policy of equality legislation. Such favourable treatment may include altering the layout of the workplace or adjusting the expectations of employees. If someone with a disability was professionally judged against the same criteria as someone without a disability, this could be seen as excluding the disabled person as they may not have the capacity to perform to the same level. Therefore, reasonable adjustments have to be put in place.

In general, people working in the United Kingdom on a part-time basis, from an agency, or on fixed-term contracts, are treated in the same manner as those on full-time, permanent contracts. This is in terms of discrimination, equality, and disability laws.

Maternity and parental leave

Under the Maternity and Parental Leave, etc. Regulations 1999, maternity leave is guaranteed to be available for a total of fifty-two weeks. The woman must have worked for that organisation for a minimum of twenty-six weeks to have the right to any paid maternity leave. The general system is that women are legally obliged to take two weeks of leave from the moment the child is born. During those two weeks, and for the following four weeks, the woman has the right to paid leave at ninety per cent of their salary. The third stage of maternity leave is thirty-three weeks with a right to statutory maternity pay, or ninety per cent of their usual salary if this is of lower value. In 2018, the statutory maternity pay is £145.18 per week. For the final thirteen weeks of maternity leave, the woman is not entitled to any pay. Individual businesses may offer different maternity packages, but this is the standard.

The mother is obliged to tell her employer about her upcoming maternity at least fifteen weeks before the due date of the child. The employer can request this notification in writing if they wish. Of course, no employee is allowed to suffer from any adverse changes to their working position, nor to be dismissed, during their absence for parental leave. The mother has the right to return to her job after twenty-six weeks of maternity leave, or to a suitable alternative position after fifty-two weeks.

Maternity regulations can apply to either carer in the case of adoption. On the other hand, the rights to fathers for paternity leave are not generally as generous as those of for mothers with maternity leave. The Paternity and Adoption Leave Regulations 2002 mean that a father can have two weeks of leave, at the statutory rate of pay (£145.18 per week in 2018). Some employers will offer full pay for one or both of these weeks. The Additional Paternity Leave Regulations 2010 have made it possible for the mother to transfer up to half of her maternity leave to her partner, in an attempt to redress the gender imbalance. Part of the reason for this was the increase in women being primary wage-earners in householders. In spite of these legal changes, however, the gender pay gap is exacerbated since women generally take more parental leave than men do.

Both parents, whether by birth or by adoption, may take additional parental leave up until their child turns five years old (or eighteen years old if the child has a disability). The limit on this additional leave is thirteen weeks and is to be unpaid. The general practice is that employees should give their employer a minimum of twenty-one days' notice to do this, and they cannot take more than four weeks a year. The parent must also take at least one week at a time, and not odd days. Regarding parental leave, the employer has the right to defer the leave for up to six months if there would be a severe disruption to the business by the employee taking such leave.

Termination of employment

All employees should have a probationary period in their new workplace. This is generally one month, though it does vary between different organisations. After their probationary period, the employee is entitled to a fair notice before dismissal. The onus is on the employer to ensure that their 'fair notice' period is agreed in the employee's contract, though the minimum is one week. After the employee has been working for two years, the notice period rises to a minimum of two weeks, and then three weeks after three years, and so on. After twelve years of service, the minimum notice period for an employer to dismiss an employee is twelve weeks. This is the most extended minimum notice period under British law. An exception to this would be if the employee were guilty of gross misconduct, in which case no notice period would be required. An employer may also pay additional pay in lieu of giving a notice period, but this usually has to be agreed with both parties.

If an employee has been working in the same business for over two years, there must be a fair reason given for their termination. Before that time, there generally does not have to be a reason given; though it is usual practice for employers to cite a particular cause for the dismissal. Employees of over two years will also be entitled to a redundancy payment if it is considered that their role is no longer necessary for the running of the business. This is set out under the Redundancy Payments Act 1965. Redundancy payments also increase with length of service, with employees under 22 years old entitled to half a weeks' pay per year worked, those aged between 22 and 40 years old entitled to one weeks' pay per year worked and those aged over 40 years old entitled to one and a half weeks' pay per year worked. Even if an employee's role has become redundant to the business, an employee still has to ensure that they follow a fair procedure for dismissal, lest they find themselves being taken to a tribunal for unfair or wrongful dismissal.

In the United Kingdom, employees do not have many options to challenge terminations of employment before they occur. To improve the situation for employees, European Union law states that employers must consult their workforce on changes to the infrastructure, including potential redundancies.

However, following the termination of a contract, if the employee believes that they have been wrongfully dismissed, they may challenge this. Such cases would be when someone is dismissed in a way that goes against the terms of their contract. Of course, if the employee has contravened their contract, they cannot claim to have been wrongfully dismissed. Notice periods would not apply to someone who broke the rules of their contract either.

Unfair dismissal is different to a wrongful dismissal. The latter is based upon someone's contract being terminated for a reason contravening the said contract, whereas the former is founded on someone being dismissed in a way that does not meet the statutory definition of fair according to the Employment Rights Act 1996. For a dismissal to be considered fair, it must be on the grounds of the employee being incapable or unqualified to complete their duties, or because the employee had demonstrated negative conduct or their role was now redundant. Another cause for fair dismissal is if the continued employment would go against another law. However, things such as being a member of a trade union, or being of a particular age or race, would not be considered fair reasons for termination of a contract.

Wage regulation

The National Minimum Wage Act 1998 means that employees over the age of 25 must earn at least £7.83 per hour (2018). For people ages 21 to 24, this figure is £7.38 per hour, for 18 to 20, it is £5.90 per hour, and for under-18s it is £4.20 per hour. These figures are all reviewed annually by the British government.

There has been controversy over elements of wage regulation in the United Kingdom. For example, if an employee can remain in their own home, but is expected to answer telephone calls, the question arises as to whether all of that time counts as hours worked. If people are allowed sleep breaks during shifts, or if they are expected to be on-call as a part of their profession, which hours are included as working hours has been queried. These questions are moot, however, as the law is clear on all of these issues. Regardless of if someone is at home or not, if they expected to complete any kind of work during a timeframe, then that all counts as working hours. If they are on-call, then that entire time counts as working hours if the employee has to remain within a reasonable vicinity of their workplace – even if the employee is asleep awaiting a possible telephone call. However, if an employee is provided with sleeping facilities at work and is taking a sleep break, the minimum wage does not apply as those hours are not included. There is an exception to this if both employer and employee agree to determine what times the employee was working for during any of these situations. In that case, they can, under mutual agreement, decide on which hours to include and therefore on what pay is owed.

Social insurance system

The Social Security Contributions and Benefits Act 1992 means that all employees are entitled to statutory sick pay. In many workplaces, staff can also earn occupational sick pay, which is a higher monetary amount that statutory sick pay. Employers must have insurance against workplace injury; a regulation enforced by the Employers' Liability (Compulsory Insurance) Act 1969.

If an adult citizen of the United Kingdom is unemployed, they may be able to claim a "jobseekers allowance", which is mainly funded through income tax and National Insurance contributions. The amount that one can claim for this in 2018 is £57.90 per week if one is aged between 18 and 24, and £73.10 per week if over 25. Someone claiming this social benefit must not be in full-time education or have an illness or disability which prevents them from working (a disability benefit is an alternative, but people cannot claim both). If the person has a romantic partner, the partner cannot be working for more than twenty-four hours a week on average. Otherwise, the claimant is to rely on their partner rather than the state. Finally, the claimant must prove that he or she is actively seeking employment, for example by providing photocopies of application forms, in order to claim.

BUSINESS ETIQUETTE IN THE UNITED KINGDOM

Punctuality

This is intentionally the first section in this chapter, as punctuality is a cornerstone to British business etiquette. Keeping to time, for business arrangements or otherwise, is valued in British society and certainly in British industry. For the people of the United Kingdom, time is often seen as an economic resource, and therefore must be adhered to. This has led to business leaders from other countries finding the British to appear rushed and flustered, but it is simply due to time consciousness.

Lateness to a business meeting is seen as incredibly impolite. If there is a genuine reason for tardiness, this will usually be accepted with an apology when you arrive at the meeting. However, if one is likely to be more than five to ten minutes late, that person should call ahead to indicate when they expect to arrive. They may even wish to suggest a postponement of the meeting. The main reason behind this is that people do not wish to be late for their next engagement, and therefore are unhappy to begin a prior one later than is necessary.

In regards to attending social business functions, lateness is seen as being more excusable. Regardless, it would be rare for business delegates to be more than fifteen minutes late to one of these.

Gift giving

Gift giving is not a standard part of British business etiquette. Offering gifts in return, if one has received a gift themselves, is good practice though. In some cases, the receipt of gifts is disallowed on legal ground, within specific industries. Of course, it must not in any way be construed as being a bribe.

If acknowledging an occasion, such as when business negotiations have been successfully concluded, then a gift may be appropriate. For traditional times, such as Christmas, it is not usual to exchange gifts in British business. Greetings cards are used, and some workplaces may operate a "Secret Santa system". This is where all of the participants' names are placed into a hat or a box and mixed up. Then, each person chooses one name from the box and doesn't tell anyone which name was picked. By picking that person's name, he/she is responsible for buying a gift for him/her.

It is unlikely to find an organisation in which everyone purchases gifts for each other.

Flowers are a gift that is used in business. Usually, this may be for an occasion of an employee or colleague, such as the birth of their child, or when someone is invited to dinner with a business associate. If using flowers as a gift, avoid using red roses or white lilies. In British culture, the former denotes romantic intentions, and the latter is a symbol of grief at bereavement.

Dress code

While some companies may have their business dress code, the standard practice is for people to wear conservative clothing when at work. Workers of either gender usually wear darker colours. Denim is not seen as acceptable in most British workplaces. Religious attire, such as *hijabs*, *kippot* and *pagris* are acceptable based on equality grounds.

Of course, many businesses provide a uniform for their staff to wear, allowing a consistency to the attire of the employees. Specific uniforms may be necessary for health and safety reasons, such as high visibility jackets for road engineers.

Furthermore, there is an increasing number of office-based businesses in which people are allowed to wear more casual clothing on Fridays. This has been the result of an attempted emulation of Dot Com Business Culture found in other parts of the world, such as California.

Corporate and social responsibilities

The importance of corporate social responsibility (CSR) is massively growing in the United Kingdom. The government supports this system through corporate tax incentives and by encouraging charitable donations by businesses.

The main themes of this involve workplace issues, community contribution, and the environment.

Concerning workplace issues, this is primarily aimed at maintaining a healthy work-life balance, while keeping to human rights and employment laws. Community contribution is about involving all stakeholders in decision making and sustaining social justice.

The main idea of the environment's involvement in CSR is about the sustainability of resources. The United Kingdom has pledged to the United Nations' Millennium Development Goals and many industrial and economic leaders in the country actively work towards achieving these.

Bribery

Corruption is low in British business culture. The United Kingdom has been proven to be regularly ranked in the top ten per cent of countries in terms of the International Corruption Perception Index, showing that British people value fairness.

The chances of having a bribe accepted are incredibly remote as the associated risks are high and, in general, British people disagree with the notion.

Meetings

In the United Kingdom, meetings often begin with a good amount of seemingly meaningless small talk (usually about the weather). This is seen as a good way to start the meeting in a harmonious manner.

Most business meetings will have preset objectives and an agenda. If anyone present at the meeting wishes to discuss something else, they must wait for what is usually the last item on the agenda – otherwise known as any other business (AOB).

Issues that arise in the meeting or suggestions for strategies, will lead to actions being made that are likely to be reviewed in the subsequent meeting.

If business cards are shared at a meeting or otherwise, it is polite to at least glance at it before putting it in your pocket. This is especially the case when meeting a new client. Not everyone will have business cards, so do not be offended if someone doesn't offer one. Out of respect, make sure that you take any offered business cards and that you take them away with you rather than discarding them in view of the person who distributed them.

Humour

This is a primary part of the British language and can certainly be found within work settings. The humour of British people can often be either sarcastic or self-deprecating, or indeed both, though it is most commonly used to help to restore amiability in an uncomfortable situation. However, one must use caution when using humour as one does not wish to offend. Moreover, some settings, such as formal meetings, would not ordinarily be considered an appropriate place for humour.

Introductions

The usual greeting for both men and women in British business is a firm handshake (not too firm though). It is very unusual for kissing on the cheek to be used. One should use the name of however someone introduces themselves. For example, if they introduce themselves with their first name, then that should be used. However, if they present themselves with a title, such as Mr Brown or Mrs Smith, then that should be used instead.

In general, the best advice is to remain formal when first meeting new business acquaintances. Ensuring that one maintains eye-contact, without outright staring, is also essential and well-received. It is also considered essential to remain in close proximity to another person during a conversation.

Socialisation

Although Brits are famous for drinking tea, many prefer coffee. Either way, it is common for colleagues to make hot drinks for each other. If one is in a working environment with a team, it is a good idea to offer to take a turn in doing this. It will show willing, and offer an opportunity for an informal chat. If you do not like to drink such drinks, it is perfectly acceptable to decline an offer. If you do want one, make sure that you state how you like it to be prepared (how much milk and sugar, if applicable).

Many work teams in the United Kingdom will extend their contact with each other beyond the workplace by going out together for lunch or going for a drink after work. This is especially common when it is a special occasion, such as a colleague's birthday or during the Christmas period. If one is invited to join with such an outing, it is courteous to accept, even if one cannot stay for long.

Indirect speech

Most British people avoid the use of direct statements of command, even in business. In general, they will opt for softer, more polite, suggestions instead through the use of indirect speech.

Some examples could be of help.

Don't say:	Use these statements instead:
I disagree with you	I see what you mean, but... I agree up to a point, but...
I think that's a bad idea	I don't think that's such a good idea
I think that's out of the question	I'm sorry, but I think that's out of the question
I don't like it	I don't really like it, I'm afraid
You need to give us a better price	I'm sorry, but we're looking for a better price
You don't understand me	I'm not making myself clear
Please send me the documents	Could you please send me the documents?

Don't say:	Use these statements instead:
You should consider the following course of action	You might like to consider the following course of action
Please sign and return the document	Would it please be possible for you to send me the signed document by the end of the week?
This clause needs renegotiating	Don't you think this clause should be renegotiated?

The use of indirect speech can be challenging to people who are not accustomed to it, or for people for whom English is not their first language. However, by using it, one can appear accommodating and approachable, rather than arrogant or rude.

Speaking about language, it must also be noted that, as a general rule, it is better to be self-deprecating than self-promotional in the United Kingdom. People who are verbally positive about themselves and their skills are easily disbelieved and disliked.

CONCLUSION

Setting up and maintaining a business in the United Kingdom is potentially easy, especially if a comparison with other European jurisdictions is made. However, the level of complexity in this varies with the size and scale of the business, plus the industry one wishes to operate in.

The United Kingdom is historically recognised as a well-established and reputable jurisdiction in which to conduct business. It's an ideal placement between the markets of the East and West, offers good transport infrastructure, uses a universally used language, plus the familiarity of business culture for many new investors makes it a highly efficient place to access world markets from.

It could be said that the British public sector that deals with business entities (mainly Companies House and HMRC) is quite friendly and willing to provide help to those cooperate, and more severe with those who breach the rules, both intentionally or unwittingly.

The implications of the Brexit referendum are yet to be determined, so it's hard to determine just how drastic the ramifications will be. Much commerce and business law that is used in the United Kingdom is borne of European Union legislation, and so it remains to be seen how much of that may change.

Nonetheless, the UK's diverse and positive attitude towards helping new businesses thrive simply cannot be ignored. If one embraces the British culture and follows the business laws and etiquette intently, there is no reason why a new foreign business cannot achieve great things.

Annex – Model Articles for private companies limited by shares

PART 1. INTERPRETATION AND LIMITATION OF LIABILITY

Defined terms

1. In the articles, unless the context requires otherwise—

"articles" means the company's articles of association;

"bankruptcy" includes individual insolvency proceedings in a jurisdiction other than England and Wales or Northern Ireland which have an effect similar to that of bankruptcy;

"chairman" has the meaning given in article 12;

"chairman of the meeting" has the meaning given in article 39;

"Companies Acts" means the Companies Acts (as defined in section 2 of the Companies Act 2006), in so far as they apply to the company;

"director" means a director of the company, and includes any person occupying the position of director, by whatever name called;

"distribution recipient" has the meaning given in article 31;

"document" includes, unless otherwise specified, any document sent or supplied in electronic form;

"electronic form" has the meaning given in section 1168 of the Companies Act 2006;

"fully paid" in relation to a share, means that the nominal value and any premium to be paid to the company in respect of that share have been paid to the company;

"hard copy form" has the meaning given in section 1168 of the Companies Act 2006;

"holder" in relation to shares means the person whose name is entered in the register of members as the holder of the shares;

"instrument" means a document in hard copy form;

"ordinary resolution" has the meaning given in section 282 of the Companies Act 2006;

"paid" means paid or credited as paid;

"participate", in relation to a directors' meeting, has the meaning given in article 10;

"proxy notice" has the meaning given in article 45;

"shareholder" means a person who is the holder of a share;

"shares" means shares in the company;

"special resolution" has the meaning given in section 283 of the Companies Act 2006;

"subsidiary" has the meaning given in section 1159 of the Companies Act 2006;

"transmittee" means a person entitled to a share by reason of the death or bankruptcy of a shareholder or otherwise by operation of law; and

"writing" means the representation or reproduction of words, symbols or other information in a visible form by any method or combination of methods, whether sent or supplied in electronic form or otherwise.

Unless the context otherwise requires, other words or expressions contained in these articles bear the same meaning as in the Companies Act 2006 as in force on the date when these articles become binding on the company.

Liability of members

2. The liability of the members is limited to the amount, if any, unpaid on the shares held by them.

PART 2. DIRECTORS

DIRECTORS' POWERS AND RESPONSIBILITIES

Directors' general authority

3. Subject to the articles, the directors are responsible for the management of the company's business, for which purpose they may exercise all the powers of the company.

Shareholders' reserve power

4.–(1) The shareholders may, by special resolution, direct the directors to take, or refrain from taking, specified action.

(2) No such special resolution invalidates anything which the directors have done before the passing of the resolution.

Directors may delegate

5.—(1) Subject to the articles, the directors may delegate any of the powers which are conferred on them under the articles—
(a) to such person or committee;
(b) by such means (including by power of attorney);
(c) to such an extent;
(d) in relation to such matters or territories; and
(e) on such terms and conditions;
as they think fit.
(2) If the directors so specify, any such delegation may authorise further delegation of the
directors' powers by any person to whom they are delegated.
(3) The directors may revoke any delegation in whole or part, or alter its terms and conditions.

Committees

6.—(1) Committees to which the directors delegate any of their powers must follow procedures which are based as far as they are applicable on those provisions of the articles which govern the taking of decisions by directors.
(2) The directors may make rules of procedure for all or any committees, which prevail over

rules derived from the articles if they are not consistent with them.

DECISION-MAKING BY DIRECTORS

Directors to take decisions collectively

7.—(1) The general rule about decision-making by directors is that any decision of the directors must be either a majority decision at a meeting or a decision taken in accordance with article 8.

(2) If—

(a) the company only has one director, and

(b) no provision of the articles requires it to have more than one director,

the general rule does not apply, and the director may take decisions without regard to any of the provisions of the articles relating to directors' decision-making.

Unanimous decisions

8.—(1) A decision of the directors is taken in accordance with this article when all eligible directors indicate to each other by any means that they share a common view on a matter.

(2) Such a decision may take the form of a resolution in writing, copies of which have been signed by each eligible director or to which each eligible director has otherwise indicated agreement in writing.

(3) References in this article to eligible directors are to directors who would have been entitled to

vote on the matter had it been proposed as a resolution at a directors' meeting.

(4) A decision may not be taken in accordance with this article if the eligible directors would not have formed a quorum at such a meeting.

Calling a directors' meeting

9.—(1) Any director may call a directors' meeting by giving notice of the meeting to the directors or by authorising the company secretary (if any) to give such notice.

(2) Notice of any directors' meeting must indicate—

(a) its proposed date and time;

(b) where it is to take place; and

(c) if it is anticipated that directors participating in the meeting will not be in the same place, how it is proposed that they should communicate with each other during the meeting.

(3) Notice of a directors' meeting must be given to each director, but need not be in writing.

(4) Notice of a directors' meeting need not be given to directors who waive their entitlement to notice of that meeting, by giving notice to that effect to the company not more than 7 days after the date on which the meeting is held. Where such notice is given after the meeting has been held, that does not affect the validity of the meeting, or of any business conducted at it.

Participation in directors' meetings

10.—(1) Subject to the articles, directors participate in a directors' meeting, or part of a

directors' meeting, when—

(a) the meeting has been called and takes place in accordance with the articles, and

(b) they can each communicate to the others any information or opinions they have on any particular item of the business of the meeting.

(2) In determining whether directors are participating in a directors' meeting, it is irrelevant where any director is or how they communicate with each other.

(3) If all the directors participating in a meeting are not in the same place, they may decide that the meeting is to be treated as taking place wherever any of them is.

Quorum for directors' meetings

11.—(1) At a directors' meeting, unless a quorum is participating, no proposal is to be voted on, except a proposal to call another meeting.

(2) The quorum for directors' meetings may be fixed from time to time by a decision of the directors, but it must never be less than two, and unless otherwise fixed it is two.

(3) If the total number of directors for the time being is less than the quorum required, the

directors must not take any decision other than a decision—

(a) to appoint further directors, or

(b) to call a general meeting so as to enable the shareholders to appoint further directors.

Chairing of directors' meetings

12.—(1) The directors may appoint a director to chair their meetings.
(2) The person so appointed for the time being is known as the chairman.
(3) The directors may terminate the chairman's appointment at any time.
(4) If the chairman is not participating in a directors' meeting within ten minutes of the time at which it was to start, the participating directors must appoint one of themselves to chair it.

Casting vote

13.—(1) If the numbers of votes for and against a proposal are equal, the chairman or other director chairing the meeting has a casting vote.
(2) But this does not apply if, in accordance with the articles, the chairman or other director is not to be counted as participating in the decision-making process for quorum or voting purposes.

Conflicts of interest

14.—(1) If a proposed decision of the directors is concerned with an actual or proposed
transaction or arrangement with the company in which a director is interested, that director is

not to be counted as participating in the decision-making process for quorum or voting purposes.

(2) But if paragraph (3) applies, a director who is interested in an actual or proposed transaction or arrangement with the company is to be counted as participating in the decision-making process for quorum and voting purposes.

(3) This paragraph applies when—

(a) the company by ordinary resolution disapplies the provision of the articles which would otherwise prevent a director from being counted as participating in the decision-making process;

(b) the director's interest cannot reasonably be regarded as likely to give rise to a conflict of interest; or

(c) the director's conflict of interest arises from a permitted cause.

(4) For the purposes of this article, the following are permitted causes—

(a) a guarantee given, or to be given, by or to a director in respect of an obligation incurred by or on behalf of the company or any of its subsidiaries;

(b) subscription, or an agreement to subscribe, for shares or other securities of the company or any of its subsidiaries, or to underwrite, sub-underwrite, or guarantee subscription for any such shares or securities; and

(c) arrangements pursuant to which benefits are made available to employees and directors or former employees and directors of the company or any of its subsidiaries which do not provide special benefits for directors or former directors.

(5) For the purposes of this article, references to proposed decisions and decision-making

processes include any directors' meeting or part of a directors' meeting.

(6) Subject to paragraph (7), if a question arises at a meeting of directors or of a committee of directors as to the right of a director to participate in the meeting (or part of the meeting) for voting or quorum purposes, the question may, before the conclusion of the meeting, be referred to the chairman whose ruling in relation to any director other than the chairman is to be final and conclusive.

(7) If any question as to the right to participate in the meeting (or part of the meeting) should arise in respect of the chairman, the question is to be decided by a decision of the directors at that meeting, for which purpose the chairman is not to be counted as participating in the meeting (or that part of the meeting) for voting or quorum purposes.

Records of decisions to be kept

15. The directors must ensure that the company keeps a record, in writing, for at least 10 years from the date of the decision recorded, of every unanimous or majority decision taken by the directors.

Directors' discretion to make further rules

16. Subject to the articles, the directors may make any rule which they think fit about how they take decisions, and about how such rules are to be recorded or communicated to directors.

APPOINTMENT OF DIRECTORS

Methods of appointing directors

17.—(1) Any person who is willing to act as a director, and is permitted by law to do so, may be appointed to be a director—
 (a) by ordinary resolution, or
 (b) by a decision of the directors.
(2) In any case where, as a result of death, the company has no shareholders and no directors, the personal representatives of the last shareholder to have died have the right, by notice in writing, to appoint a person to be a director.
(3) For the purposes of paragraph (2), where 2 or more shareholders die in circumstances
rendering it uncertain who was the last to die, a younger shareholder is deemed to have survived an older shareholder.

Termination of director's appointment

18. A person ceases to be a director as soon as—

(a) that person ceases to be a director by virtue of any provision of the Companies Act 2006 or is prohibited from being a director by law;

(b) a bankruptcy order is made against that person;

(c) a composition is made with that person's creditors generally in satisfaction of that person's debts;

(d) a registered medical practitioner who is treating that person gives a written opinion to the company stating that that person has become physically or mentally incapable of acting as a director and may remain so for more than three months;

(e) by reason of that person's mental health, a court makes an order which wholly or partly prevents that person from personally exercising any powers or rights which that person would otherwise have;

(f) notification is received by the company from the director that the director is resigning from office, and such resignation has taken effect in accordance with its terms.

Directors' remuneration

19.—(1) Directors may undertake any services for the company that the directors decide.

(2) Directors are entitled to such remuneration as the directors determine—

(a) for their services to the company as directors, and

(b) for any other service which they undertake for the company.

(3) Subject to the articles, a director's remuneration may—

(a) take any form, and

(b) include any arrangements in connection with the payment of a pension, allowance or gratuity, or any death, sickness or disability benefits, to or in respect of that director.

(4) Unless the directors decide otherwise, directors' remuneration accrues from day to day.

(5) Unless the directors decide otherwise, directors are not accountable to the company for any remuneration which they receive as directors or other officers or employees of the company's subsidiaries or of any other body corporate in which the company is interested.

Directors' expenses

20. The company may pay any reasonable expenses which the directors properly incur in connection with their attendance at—

(a) meetings of directors or committees of directors,

(b) general meetings, or

(c) separate meetings of the holders of any class of shares or of debentures of the company, or otherwise in connection with the exercise of their powers and the discharge of their responsibilities in relation to the company.

PART 3. SHARES AND DISTRIBUTIONS

SHARES

All shares to be fully paid up

21.—(1) No share is to be issued for less than the aggregate of its nominal value and any premium to be paid to the company in consideration for its issue.

(2) This does not apply to shares taken on the formation of the company by the subscribers to the company's memorandum.

Powers to issue different classes of share

22.—(1) Subject to the articles, but without prejudice to the rights attached to any existing share, the company may issue shares with such rights or restrictions as may be determined by ordinary resolution.

(2) The company may issue shares which are to be redeemed, or are liable to be redeemed at the option of the company or the holder, and the directors may determine the terms, conditions and manner of redemption of any such shares.

Company not bound by less than absolute interests

23. Except as required by law, no person is to be recognised by the company as holding any share upon any trust, and except as otherwise required by law or the articles, the company is not in any way to be bound by or recognise any interest in a share other than the holder's absolute ownership of it and all the rights attaching to it.

Share certificates

24.—(1) The company must issue each shareholder, free of charge, with one or more certificates in respect of the shares which that shareholder holds.

(2) Every certificate must specify—

(a) in respect of how many shares, of what class, it is issued;

(b) the nominal value of those shares;

(c) that the shares are fully paid; and

(d) any distinguishing numbers assigned to them.

(3) No certificate may be issued in respect of shares of more than one class.

(4) If more than one person holds a share, only one certificate may be issued in respect of it.

(5) Certificates must—

(a) have affixed to them the company's common seal, or

(b) be otherwise executed in accordance with the Companies Acts.

Replacement share certificates

25.—(1) If a certificate issued in respect of a shareholder's shares is—

(a) damaged or defaced, or

(b) said to be lost, stolen or destroyed,

that shareholder is entitled to be issued with a replacement certificate in respect of the same shares.

(2) A shareholder exercising the right to be issued with such a replacement certificate—

(a) may at the same time exercise the right to be issued with a single certificate or separate certificates;

(b) must return the certificate which is to be replaced to the company if it is damaged or defaced; and

(c) must comply with such conditions as to evidence, indemnity and the payment of a reasonable fee as the directors decide.

Share transfers

26.—(1) Shares may be transferred by means of an instrument of transfer in any usual form or any other form approved by the directors, which is executed by or on behalf of the transferor.

(2) No fee may be charged for registering any instrument of transfer or other document relating to or affecting the title to any share.

(3) The company may retain any instrument of transfer which is registered.

(4) The transferor remains the holder of a share until the transferee's name is entered in the register of members as holder of it.

(5) The directors may refuse to register the transfer of a share, and if they do so, the instrument of transfer must be returned to the transferee with

the notice of refusal unless they suspect that the proposed transfer may be fraudulent.

Transmission of shares

27.—(1) If title to a share passes to a transmittee, the company may only recognise the transmittee as having any title to that share.

(2) A transmittee who produces such evidence of entitlement to shares as the directors may properly require—

(a) may, subject to the articles, choose either to become the holder of those shares or to have them transferred to another person, and

(b) subject to the articles, and pending any transfer of the shares to another person, has the same rights as the holder had.

(3) But transmittees do not have the right to attend or vote at a general meeting, or agree to a proposed written resolution, in respect of shares to which they are entitled, by reason of the holder's death or bankruptcy or otherwise, unless they become the holders of those shares.

Exercise of transmittees' rights

28.—(1) Transmittees who wish to become the holders of shares to which they have become entitled must notify the company in writing of that wish.

(2) If the transmittee wishes to have a share transferred to another person, the transmittee must execute an instrument of transfer in respect of it.

(3) Any transfer made or executed under this article is to be treated as if it were made or executed by the person from whom the transmittee has derived rights in respect of the share, and as if the event which gave rise to the transmission had not occurred.

Transmittees bound by prior notices

29. If a notice is given to a shareholder in respect of shares and a transmittee is entitled to those shares, the transmittee is bound by the notice if it was given to the shareholder before the transmittee's name has been entered in the register of members.

DIVIDENDS AND OTHER DISTRIBUTIONS

Procedure for declaring dividends

30.—(1) The company may by ordinary resolution declare dividends, and the directors may decide to pay interim dividends.

(2) A dividend must not be declared unless the directors have made a recommendation as to its amount. Such a dividend must not exceed the amount recommended by the directors.

(3) No dividend may be declared or paid unless it is in accordance with shareholders' respective rights.

(4) Unless the shareholders' resolution to declare or directors' decision to pay a dividend, or the terms on which shares are issued, specify otherwise, it must be paid by reference to each shareholder's

holding of shares on the date of the resolution or decision to declare or pay it.

(5) If the company's share capital is divided into different classes, no interim dividend may be paid on shares carrying deferred or non-preferred rights if, at the time of payment, any preferential dividend is in arrear.

(6) The directors may pay at intervals any dividend payable at a fixed rate if it appears to them that the profits available for distribution justify the payment.

(7) If the directors act in good faith, they do not incur any liability to the holders of shares

conferring preferred rights for any loss they may suffer by the lawful payment of an interim dividend on shares with deferred or non-preferred rights.

Payment of dividends and other distributions

31.—(1) Where a dividend or other sum which is a distribution is payable in respect of a share, it must be paid by one or more of the following means—

(a) transfer to a bank or building society account specified by the distribution recipient either in writing or as the directors may otherwise decide;

(b) sending a cheque made payable to the distribution recipient by post to the distribution recipient at the distribution recipient's registered address (if the distribution recipient is a holder of the share), or (in any other case) to an address specified by the distribution recipient either in writing or as the directors may otherwise decide;

(c) sending a cheque made payable to such person by post to such person at such address as the distribution recipient has specified either in writing or as the directors may otherwise decide; or

(d) any other means of payment as the directors agree with the distribution recipient either in writing or by such other means as the directors decide.

(2) In the articles, "the distribution recipient" means, in respect of a share in respect of which a dividend or other sum is payable—

(a) the holder of the share; or

(b) if the share has two or more joint holders, whichever of them is named first in the register of members; or

(c) if the holder is no longer entitled to the share by reason of death or bankruptcy, or otherwise by operation of law, the transmittee.

No interest on distributions

32. The company may not pay interest on any dividend or other sum payable in respect of a share unless otherwise provided by—

(a) the terms on which the share was issued, or

(b) the provisions of another agreement between the holder of that share and the company.

Unclaimed distributions

33.—(1) All dividends or other sums which are—

(a) payable in respect of shares, and

(b) unclaimed after having been declared or become payable,

may be invested or otherwise made use of by the directors for the benefit of the company until claimed.

(2) The payment of any such dividend or other sum into a separate account does not make the company a trustee in respect of it.

(3) If—

(a) twelve years have passed from the date on which a dividend or other sum became due for payment, and

(b) the distribution recipient has not claimed it,

the distribution recipient is no longer entitled to that dividend or other sum and it ceases to remain owing by the company.

Non-cash distributions

34.—(1) Subject to the terms of issue of the share in question, the company may, by ordinary resolution on the recommendation of the directors, decide to pay all or part of a dividend or other distribution payable in respect of a share by transferring non-cash assets of equivalent value (including, without limitation, shares or other securities in any company).

(2) For the purposes of paying a non-cash distribution, the directors may make whatever arrangements they think fit, including, where any difficulty arises regarding the distribution—

(a) fixing the value of any assets;

(b) paying cash to any distribution recipient on the basis of that value in order to adjust the rights of recipients; and

(c) vesting any assets in trustees.

Waiver of distributions

35. Distribution recipients may waive their entitlement to a dividend or other distribution payable in respect of a share by giving the company notice in writing to that effect, but if—

(a) the share has more than one holder, or

(b) more than one person is entitled to the share, whether by reason of the death or

(c) bankruptcy of one or more joint holders, or otherwise,

the notice is not effective unless it is expressed to be given, and signed, by all the holders or persons otherwise entitled to the share.

CAPITALISATION OF PROFITS

Authority to capitalise and appropriation of capitalised sums

36.—(1) Subject to the articles, the directors may, if they are so authorised by an ordinary resolution—

(a) decide to capitalise any profits of the company (whether or not they are available for distribution) which are not required for paying a preferential dividend, or any sum standing to the credit of the company's share premium account or capital redemption reserve; and

(b) appropriate any sum which they so decide to capitalise (a "capitalised sum") to the persons who would have been entitled to it if it were distributed by way of dividend (the "persons entitled") and in the same proportions.

(2) Capitalised sums must be applied—

(a) on behalf of the persons entitled, and

(b) in the same proportions as a dividend would have been distributed to them.

(3) Any capitalised sum may be applied in paying up new shares of a nominal amount equal to the capitalised sum which are then allotted credited as fully paid to the persons entitled or as they may direct.

(4) A capitalised sum which was appropriated from profits available for distribution may be applied in paying up new debentures of the company which are then allotted credited as fully paid to the persons entitled or as they may direct.

(5) Subject to the articles the directors may—

(a) apply capitalised sums in accordance with paragraphs (3) and (4) partly in one way and partly in another;

(b) make such arrangements as they think fit to deal with shares or debentures becoming distributable in fractions under this article (including the issuing of fractional certificates or the making of cash payments); and

(c) authorise any person to enter into an agreement with the company on behalf of all the persons entitled which is binding on them in respect of the allotment of shares and debentures to them under this article.

PART 4. DECISION-MAKING BY SHAREHOLDERS

ORGANISATION OF GENERAL MEETINGS

Attendance and speaking at general meetings

37.—(1) A person is able to exercise the right to speak at a general meeting when that person is in a position to communicate to all those attending the meeting, during the meeting, any information or opinions which that person has on the business of the meeting.

(2) A person is able to exercise the right to vote at a general meeting when—

(a) that person is able to vote, during the meeting, on resolutions put to the vote at the meeting, and

(b) that person's vote can be taken into account in determining whether or not such

resolutions are passed at the same time as the votes of all the other persons attending the meeting.

(3) The directors may make whatever arrangements they consider appropriate to enable those attending a general meeting to exercise their rights to speak or vote at it.

(4) In determining attendance at a general meeting, it is immaterial whether any two or more members attending it are in the same place as each other.

(5) Two or more persons who are not in the same place as each other attend a general meeting if their circumstances are such that if they have (or were to have) rights to speak and vote at that meeting, they are (or would be) able to exercise them.

Quorum for general meetings

38. No business other than the appointment of the chairman of the meeting is to be transacted at a general meeting if the persons attending it do not constitute a quorum.

Chairing general meetings

39.—(1) If the directors have appointed a chairman, the chairman shall chair general meetings if present and willing to do so.

(2) If the directors have not appointed a chairman, or if the chairman is unwilling to chair the meeting or is not present within ten minutes of the time at which a meeting was due to start—

(a) the directors present, or

(b) (if no directors are present), the meeting,

must appoint a director or shareholder to chair the meeting, and the appointment of the chairman of the meeting must be the first business of the meeting.

(3) The person chairing a meeting in accordance with this article is referred to as "the chairman of the meeting".

Attendance and speaking by directors and non-shareholders

40.—(1) Directors may attend and speak at general meetings, whether or not they are shareholders.

(2) The chairman of the meeting may permit other persons who are not—

(a) shareholders of the company, or

(b) otherwise entitled to exercise the rights of shareholders in relation to general meetings,

to attend and speak at a general meeting.

Adjournment

41.—(1) If the persons attending a general meeting within half an hour of the time at which the meeting was due to start do not constitute a quorum, or if during a meeting a quorum ceases to be present, the chairman of the meeting must adjourn it.

(2) The chairman of the meeting may adjourn a general meeting at which a quorum is present if—

(a) the meeting consents to an adjournment, or

(b) it appears to the chairman of the meeting that an adjournment is necessary to protect the safety of any person attending the meeting or ensure that the business of the meeting is conducted in an orderly manner.

(3) The chairman of the meeting must adjourn a general meeting if directed to do so by the meeting.

(4) When adjourning a general meeting, the chairman of the meeting must—

(a) either specify the time and place to which it is adjourned or state that it is to continue at a time and place to be fixed by the directors, and

(b) have regard to any directions as to the time and place of any adjournment which have been given by the meeting.

(5) If the continuation of an adjourned meeting is to take place more than 14 days after it was adjourned, the company must give at least 7 clear days' notice of it (that is, excluding the day of the adjourned meeting and the day on which the notice is given)—

(a) to the same persons to whom notice of the company's general meetings is required to be given, and

(b) containing the same information which such notice is required to contain.

(6) No business may be transacted at an adjourned general meeting which could not properly have been transacted at the meeting if the adjournment had not taken place.

VOTING AT GENERAL MEETINGS

Voting: general

42. A resolution put to the vote of a general meeting must be decided on a show of hands unless a poll is duly demanded in accordance with the articles.

Errors and disputes

43.—(1) No objection may be raised to the qualification of any person voting at a general meeting except at the meeting or adjourned meeting at which the vote objected to is tendered, and every vote not disallowed at the meeting is valid.

(2) Any such objection must be referred to the chairman of the meeting, whose decision is final.

Poll votes

44.—(1) A poll on a resolution may be demanded—

(a) in advance of the general meeting where it is to be put to the vote, or

(b) at a general meeting, either before a show of hands on that resolution or immediately after the result of a show of hands on that resolution is declared.

(2) A poll may be demanded by—

(a) the chairman of the meeting;

(b) the directors;

(c) two or more persons having the right to vote on the resolution; or

(d) a person or persons representing not less than one tenth of the total voting rights of all the shareholders having the right to vote on the resolution.

(3) A demand for a poll may be withdrawn if—

(a) the poll has not yet been taken, and

(b) the chairman of the meeting consents to the withdrawal.

(4) Polls must be taken immediately and in such manner as the chairman of the meeting directs.

Content of proxy notices

45.—(1) Proxies may only validly be appointed by a notice in writing (a "proxy notice")
which—

(a) states the name and address of the shareholder appointing the proxy;

(b) identifies the person appointed to be that shareholder's proxy and the general meeting in relation to which that person is appointed;

(c) is signed by or on behalf of the shareholder appointing the proxy, or is authenticated in such manner as the directors may determine; and

(d) is delivered to the company in accordance with the articles and any instructions contained in the notice of the general meeting to which they relate.

(2) The company may require proxy notices to be delivered in a particular form, and may specify different forms for different purposes.

(3) Proxy notices may specify how the proxy appointed under them is to vote (or that the proxy is to abstain from voting) on one or more resolutions.

(4) Unless a proxy notice indicates otherwise, it must be treated as—

(a) allowing the person appointed under it as a proxy discretion as to how to vote on any ancillary or procedural resolutions put to the meeting, and

(b) appointing that person as a proxy in relation to any adjournment of the general meeting to which it relates as well as the meeting itself.

Delivery of proxy notices

46.—(1) A person who is entitled to attend, speak or vote (either on a show of hands or on a poll) at a general meeting remains so entitled in respect of that meeting or any adjournment of it, even though a valid proxy notice has been delivered to the company by or on behalf of that person.

(2) An appointment under a proxy notice may be revoked by delivering to the company a notice in writing given by or on behalf of the person by whom or on whose behalf the proxy notice was given.

(3) A notice revoking a proxy appointment only takes effect if it is delivered before the start of the meeting or adjourned meeting to which it relates.

(4) If a proxy notice is not executed by the person appointing the proxy, it must be accompanied by written evidence of the authority of the person who executed it to execute it on the appointor's behalf.

Amendments to resolutions

47.—(1) An ordinary resolution to be proposed at a general meeting may be amended by ordinary resolution if—

(a) notice of the proposed amendment is given to the company in writing by a person entitled to vote at the general meeting at which it is to be proposed not less than 48 hours before the meeting is to take place (or such later time as the chairman of the meeting may determine), and

(b) the proposed amendment does not, in the reasonable opinion of the chairman of the meeting, materially alter the scope of the resolution.

(2) A special resolution to be proposed at a general meeting may be amended by ordinary resolution, if—

(a) the chairman of the meeting proposes the amendment at the general meeting at which the resolution is to be proposed, and

(b) the amendment does not go beyond what is necessary to correct a grammatical or other non-substantive error in the resolution.

(3) If the chairman of the meeting, acting in good faith, wrongly decides that an amendment to a resolution is out of order, the chairman's error does not invalidate the vote on that resolution.

PART 5. ADMINISTRATIVE ARRANGEMENTS

Means of communication to be used

48.—(1) Subject to the articles, anything sent or supplied by or to the company under the articles may be sent or supplied in any way in which the Companies Act 2006 provides for documents or information which are authorised or required by any provision of that Act to be sent or supplied by or to the company.

(2) Subject to the articles, any notice or document to be sent or supplied to a director in connection with the taking of decisions by directors may also be sent or supplied by the means by which that director has asked to be sent or supplied with such notices or documents for the time being.

(3) A director may agree with the company that notices or documents sent to that director in a particular way are to be deemed to have been received within a specified time of their being sent, and for the specified time to be less than 48 hours.

Company seals

49.—(1) Any common seal may only be used by the authority of the directors.

(2) The directors may decide by what means and in what form any common seal is to be used.

(3) Unless otherwise decided by the directors, if the company has a common seal and it is affixed to a document, the document must also be

signed by at least one authorised person in the presence of a witness who attests the signature.

(4) For the purposes of this article, an authorised person is—

(a) any director of the company;

(b) the company secretary (if any); or

(c) any person authorised by the directors for the purpose of signing documents to which the common seal is applied.

No right to inspect accounts and other records

50. Except as provided by law or authorised by the directors or an ordinary resolution of the company, no person is entitled to inspect any of the company's accounting or other records or documents merely by virtue of being a shareholder.

Provision for employees on cessation of business

51. The directors may decide to make provision for the benefit of persons employed or formerly employed by the company or any of its subsidiaries (other than a director or former director or shadow director) in connection with the cessation or transfer to any person of the whole or part of the undertaking of the company or that subsidiary.

DIRECTORS' INDEMNITY AND INSURANCE

Indemnity

52.—(1) Subject to paragraph (2), a relevant director of the company or an associated company may be indemnified out of the company's assets against—

(a) any liability incurred by that director in connection with any negligence, default, breach of duty or breach of trust in relation to the company or an associated company,

(b) any liability incurred by that director in connection with the activities of the company or an associated company in its capacity as a trustee of an occupational pension scheme (as defined in section 235(6) of the Companies Act 2006),

(c) any other liability incurred by that director as an officer of the company or an associated company.

(2) This article does not authorise any indemnity which would be prohibited or rendered void by any provision of the Companies Acts or by any other provision of law.

(3) In this article—

(a) companies are associated if one is a subsidiary of the other or both are subsidiaries of the same body corporate, and

(b) a "relevant director" means any director or former director of the company or an associated company.

Insurance

53.—(1) The directors may decide to purchase and maintain insurance, at the expense of the company, for the benefit of any relevant director in respect of any relevant loss.

(2) In this article—

(a) a "relevant director" means any director or former director of the company or an associated company,

(b) a "relevant loss" means any loss or liability which has been or may be incurred by a relevant director in connection with that director's duties or powers in relation to the company, any associated company or any pension fund or employees' share scheme of the company or associated company, and

(c) companies are associated if one is a subsidiary of the other or both are subsidiaries of the same body corporate.

Acknowledgments

This work would not have been possible without the support of all of those with whom I have had the pleasure to work during this and other related projects.

I am especially indebted to my colleagues Martin J. McCoy and Harrison O'Brien — they actively provide me with the protected time to pursue those goals. I would like to thank Daryl Charman for his constructive criticism of the manuscript.

Nobody is more important to me than the members of my family. I would like to thank my father, David, and my brother Samuel for their steady support, wisdom and endless patience. They, together with the memory of my loved mother Anna Maria, continuously provide me unending inspiration.

www.ingramcontent.com/pod-product-compliance
Lightning Source LLC
Chambersburg PA
CBHW020424220526
45464CB00002B/557